DELIVERANCE
for CHILDREN
& TEENS

BY BILL BANKS

DELIVERANCE FOR CHILDREN & TEENS
by Bill Banks

ISBN 10: 0-89228-034-4
ISBN 13: 978-089228-034-6

Copyright © 1985. Revised 2013.
Impact Christian Books

IMPACT CHRISTIAN BOOKS, INC.
332 Leffingwell Ave., Suite 101
Kirkwood, MO 63122

WWW.IMPACTCHRISTIANBOOKS.COM

All scripture quotations are from the KING JAMES VERSION of the Bible unless otherwise noted.

Scripture quotations identified NASB are from the New American Standard Bible® (NASB), Copyright © 1960, 1962, 1963, 1968, 1971, 1972, 1973, 1975, 1977, 1995 by The Lockman Foundation. Used by permission. www.Lockman.org.

ALL RIGHTS RESERVED

CONTENTS

FOREWORD

I have known Bill Banks and his family for many years. I have witnessed firsthand his compassionate ministry to hurting people and have seen the powerful results.

When I began my closer walk with the Lord in his prayer room November 11th of 1980, I did not realize how long the process would be that we as Christians must undergo if we are to mature. One aspect of Christianity that we must recognize is that once we have accepted Jesus as our Lord and Savior, the problems do not cease but may become increasingly more intense. As the Holy Spirit continues to work in our lives, He shows us that Satan is truly active in this world; part of Jesus Christ's ministry was to expose the lies of Satan and to free us from them.

Children are susceptible to the lies of Satan, and our society with its social and moral values at question, provides fertile ground for the entrance of demons. Children are constantly processing new information and sometimes cannot distinguish truth from counterfeit.

As an oral and maxillofacial surgeon, I am at times called upon to perform reconstructive facial surgery on young patients who have facial abnormalities. Usually this type of surgery brings about a favorable facial appearance. I have seen young people who were so self-conscious about their facial appearance that they had become withdrawn. Perhaps their peers had made remarks regarding their appearance and caused these young people to believe that they were socially unacceptable. The surgical correction often brings about a positive facial appearance which in turn allows a release of the patient's personality. They are thus able to enjoy the freedom of their personality which had previously been suppressed because of their self-perception.

I recently had a conversation with a young patient who had experienced it all, alcohol, drugs, the fast track life, and had even undergone an abortion. I was appalled by the total lack in her of any moral standard. She was unable to resist sin, because she had no basis upon which to make a stand. I suspect she is probably typical of many of our troubled youth, who don't have a reason to resist, nor have they yet met the true Standard.

When a young person accepts Jesus Christ into his life, Jesus takes the twisted, wounded personality and creates a new person — beautiful, free and healthy. As an individual submits to Him, Jesus takes away the self-consciousness and replaces it with His kind of confidence. He also desires to free the individual from Satan and his demons. The young Christian must continue to mature and not allow his "house" to remain empty but to fill it with God's word, for a house that is empty will not remain so (MAT. 12:23–24). Thus, I wholeheartedly recommend this book to parents and those who wish to be able to engage in spiritual warfare.

– **Dr. James Wellman** (Retired)

Author's Introduction

I am especially delighted to have the foreword to this book written by such a fine surgeon and facial reconstructionist as my good Christian friend, Dr. Jim Wellman. In many ways his work and the work of ministering in deliverance are similar. He through his skill seeks to remove what is perceived as external ugliness, and we in ministering deliverance strive to remove what are the inward scars and disfigurements, real or perceived, caused by the Enemy and his demonic influences.

I also acknowledge my indebtedness to all those who have gone before in prior centuries as well as my contemporaries who have prayerfully sought God for answers and have subsequently shared the truths revealed to them. As Maxwell Whyte (a dear brother in the Lord and forerunner in the field of deliverance, who went to his reward this year) was kind enough to write in regard to *Power for Deliverance*, "these truths will significantly contribute to the body of knowledge about deliverance." It is both my desire and my prayer that this book might do the same.

This book is not written from a position of superior knowledge; we do not have all the answers concerning deliverance for children. Rather, it is written in order that we might share some relevant truths which the Lord has allowed us to observe over the past eighteen years of ministry. It is also not written from the vantage point of being perfect parents. We are quick to admit that we made our share of mistakes as parents. However, in spite of our shortcomings, we have been blessed with two fine Christian sons, now young adults, in whom we are "well pleased."

Many friends have commented that my wife and I were fortunate to have come into all this (a deeper relationship with the Lord) at a time when our two sons were still small, and in their formative years. It was exciting to see them praying for their friends, and even adults, before they were four years old. It may have been a result of their sincere, bold, childlike faith that their prayers, especially for healing, were often speedily answered. However, even though they were blessed with such an early relationship with the Lord, they weren't spared from all trauma. My bout with terminal cancer, when they were just one-and-a-half and three-and-a-half, was traumatic but we felt at the time they were too young to comprehend. As we would learn, it in fact caused deep wounds to their souls.

In spite of the early footholds, which Satan may have obtained in the lives of your children, don't despair. There is no case too difficult, nor a soul so far lost, that the Lord cannot save. It is His desire and purpose to deliver all children and teenagers from demonic bondages.

We pray that the cases presented in this book are an encouragement for you to invite Jesus into your family situation, in order for Him to fulfill His words to you:

> " ... whosoever shall call on the name of the Lord shall be delivered: for in mount Zion and in Jerusalem shall be deliverance, ... and in the remnant whom the Lord shall call."
>
> JOEL 2:32

The simple procedures discussed in this book work well, for they are His and they are based upon His Word. A teacher in a local Charismatic Christian school once called me asking for guidance as to how to minister to a tormented child in her class. She said, "I'm sure his parents don't believe in demons, or even that he could have one, but he is emotionally disturbed and I know the fears that he has are unnatural. There has been a discussion of removing him from this school and putting him in an institution. I can't bring him to you, for the parents wouldn't permit it, but I do want to help him. What can I do?"

I briefly shared with her a few of the ministry techniques which are explained in this book, such as silently praying over him, binding the spirits that she recognized, praying in the Spirit for him, and commanding the spirits to leave him. She called a month later with a "glory report," of a boy now normal and no longer troubled. So these principles do work, and they are transferable.

We share these truths in the hope that they will help other parents learn techniques of spiritual warfare. We wish for parents to avoid the pain of children lost to rebellion or other of Satan's devices. By addressing problems early in children's lives, parents (and their children) may be spared the heartbreak of broken, wasted, maimed or impaired lives due to demonic strongholds. Instead, they may come to know the joy that God intended for children to bring to parents; and *to know* that there is the power in Jesus to bring deliverance to your child!

– Bill Banks

Books & Compact Discs
BY BILL & SUE BANKS

BOOKS - *ON PHYSICAL HEALING*

Alive Again! - *48 Hours to Live with Terminal Cancer*

Overcoming Blocks to Healing

Three Kinds of Faith for Healing

BOOKS - *DELIVERANCE AND HEALING OF THE MIND, WILL, EMOTIONS*

The Power for Deliverance (Songs of Deliverance)

Breaking Unhealthy Soul Ties

STUDY GUIDE - Breaking Unhealthy Soul Ties

Ministering to Abortion's Aftermath

Deliverance for Children & Teens

The Little Skunk - *A Children's Book on Deliverance*

Deliverance from Fat & Eating Disorders

Shame Free! - *Have You Been Maimed by Shame?*

BOOKS - *ON THE DEEPER THINGS OF GOD*

The Heavens Declare - *Jesus Christ Prophesied in the Stars*

A Skeptic Discover Angels are Real - *11 Miraculous Angel Testimonies*

How to Tap into the Wisdom of God

Discernment: God's Inner Guidance for Believers

COMPACT DISCS - *AUDIO SERIES*

Healing is for Today! (14 CDs)

Deliverance: Setting the Captives Free (11 CDs)

The Baptism in the Holy Spirit (7 CDs)

Spiritual Warfare (7 CDs)

The Overcoming Power of Prayer (9 CDs)

The Heavens Declare Teaching Series (13 CDs)

Reincarnation - The Biblical Answer (3 CDs)

The Precious Blood of Jesus (2 CDs)

On Salvation & The Baptism in the Holy Spirit (1 CD)

How I Was Healed of Cancer (1 CD)

ACKNOWLEDGMENT

I wish to express my indebtedness to my wife, Sue, for her keen insights and helpful comments, and to my two sons who have graciously assisted and permitted the sharing of their own battles and victories.

I am also extremely grateful to Pam Miltenberger who has generously and competently reviewed my grammar and punctuation, and added several helpful insights.

Finally, I am eternally in debt to the Holy Spirit who has strengthened me, and again, quickened my mortal body. The enemy has strongly opposed this manuscript, delaying its completion by attempting to take my life, and having me hospitalized for the greater part of 1988. However, the Lord has defeated his efforts, and overcome his hindrances, permitting the belated completion of this book which I trust will be an instrument for His glory and the extension of His kingdom.

LETTER FROM A BIBLE TEACHER

As a Bible teacher I am frequently at a loss to know what books to give people who want to know about deliverance. Derek Prince and Don Basham long ago wrote introductions, but a handbook for how-to has long been overdue. Bill Banks' book *Ministering To Abortion's Aftermath* written several years ago has many insights into the workings of the demonic kingdom. This new book on children will enable anyone to pray for his or her own child.

I've seen Bill in action. I have prayed with him and received ministry from him. He is balanced, Scriptural, but most of all motivated by the love he says is "God's greatest power tool." This is the most practical book yet written on deliverance for children and teens. It will help usher in God's mighty move today to set His people free. He is coming for a church without "spot or blemish."

- Pam Miltenberger

PART ONE

HOW DEMONS ENTER

"AND IT SHALL COME TO PASS, THAT WHOSOEVER SHALL CALL ON THE NAME OF THE LORD SHALL BE *DELIVERED*: FOR IN MOUNT ZION AND IN JERUSALEM SHALL BE *DELIVERANCE*, AS THE LORD HATH SAID, AND IN THE REMNANT WHOM THE LORD SHALL CALL."

JOEL 2:32

"FOR THE PROMISE IS UNTO YOU, AND TO YOUR CHILDREN, AND TO ALL THAT ARE AFAR OFF, EVEN AS MANY AS THE LORD OUR GOD SHALL CALL."

ACTS 2:39

HOW DEMONS ENTER:
GATES THROUGH WHICH DEMONS ENTER

For years there has been great need for a book that links deliverance for children with discipline and upbringing. Today's children are being exposed to all forms of aberrant behavior, and parents are losing control by the influence of peer groups at an alarming rate. The tragedy resulting from neglecting the topic of deliverance for children unfortunately is to be seen in many Christian homes where parents are trying to establish a credible witness in their communities while their children's behavior slanders their attempt.

Often parents come to us for help, knowing that their child is under the influence of an abnormal spirit, but are unwilling to mention the possibility to their child, whom they fear could be frightened by the subject. Indeed, if parents are constantly "demon-hunting," their children will probably become warped.

This book is our way of introducing the subject of deliverance for children in a balanced fashion, so that common sense discipline becomes a part of the process. We have found over the last eighteen years, that the mixture of love, discipline, and deliverance have gotten us through some very rough spots in raising our own sons. The rule of thumb in any deliverance situation is that deliverance is necessary only when common sense, consistent discipline or counseling fails. Relieving a child of demonic fears, and other types of spiritual baggage, can prevent him or her from becoming a dysfunctional adult.

When ministering deliverance to children, one frequently encounters tormenting, troubling, and vexing spirits just as Jesus did in the case of the Syrophoenician woman's daughter (Matt. 15:22ff).

It is, of course, easier for us to accept the need for deliverance in the case of an alcoholic or a drug addict than in the case of an innocent child.

Many adults who have come to us desiring deliverance had problems *originating in childhood*; they either picked up, or had a door opened for, demonic spirits when they were most vulnerable. Thus, the importance of ministering deliverance to children is clearly seen in the problems which can arise later in life. What otherwise would become a serious problem in adult life can be counteracted in childhood, before deep personality distortions can become established.

It has been our experience, as Scripture supports, that all demonic entry is gained either as a result of the individual's own choices (today or in generations past), or as a result of wounds to the human soul. Infants and toddlers are too young to knowingly sin; the age at which the child willfully sins varies with each individual. Therefore the child is made vulnerable to demonic invasion from causes other than his or her own willful sin. These include actions against the child, lack of action on behalf of the child, accidents, and in general, traumatic or fearful events. That the child is innocent or undeserving of such occurrences is, unfortunately, no more protection for the child than would innocence protect him or her from mistreatment by an abusive parent, or from a hereditary disease.

It is important to remember that a Christian can be sincere and in love with Jesus, while also being tormented or afflicted with evil spirits in some area of life. It is in the same way an innocent child can be afflicted by a spirit of physical infirmity (MARK 9:25).

The child in a healthy family unit is living to a certain degree in a force field of spiritual protection. For him (or her) it can be like living within a bubble that shields from harm and provides an environment of safety, peace, and sense of wellbeing. The child feels good, surrounded and warmed by the love of his or her parents.

If the family unit is broken, or threatened by death or divorce, the bubble of protection can be destroyed. The shield appears to develop cracks when threatened, and to burst when the family unit is broken. The result for the child can be, in certain situations, a loss of the sense of well-being, peace and comfort. The child may begin to sense (subconsciously or spiritually, even if too young to mentally comprehend the situation) that he or she is not safe. Frequently, the child in a turbulent situation becomes vulnerable to nightmares, fears and torments.

The most common fears experienced by small children tend to underscore the validity of our analysis: fear of being abandoned (being unwanted by parents or deserted by them), fear of being alone (wanting the feeling of comfort and security of having parents physically present); fear of being lost (separated from parents); fear of being kidnapped (being forcibly separated from parents). Then there are fears of the unknown, like those associated with bad dreams or nightmares, bullies, monsters, teachers, and of confinement in close quarters. These are all fears from which the child would expect his loving parents to protect him.

The nature and severity of the actions of a child with demonic issues increase in intensity and danger with age. For example, a three year old would hardly be apt to be a thief, lacking physical strength and opportunity to do so. However, in some cases, the root spirit of the *fear of poverty* can be hidden within, waiting for a certain time to manifest as stealing.

Demons can enter in a variety of ways. It is important to consider these areas of vulnerability, and to highlight specific "gates" or doorways through which spirits can enter. Our goal in this section is to provide some assistance in discovering the spiritual root of a child's problem.

Love is a powerful tool. Deliverance is effectively ministered in love. We need to assure the child that we, the ones ministering, love them, that Jesus loves them and that their parents or family loves them.

1.

Gates of the Senses

Spirits often enter through the gate of the senses. Each of the five senses provides a means of receiving knowledge, good or evil, and an opening that Satan can sometimes utilize to allow evil spirits to enter.

Eye Gate – For example, spirits of pornography and murder may enter through viewing actual events or through seeing movies. When we look at things we know we should not, an opening or "place" may be given to the devil — our mortal enemy. David looked sinfully upon Bathsheba, and his looking led to lust and eventually to murder, and resulted, among other things, in the loss of his child (2 Samuel 11). Ephesians 4:27 warns to not "give place to the devil."

Ear Gate – Adults may remember being frightened by radio theater or a recording of sounds intended to scare. By hearing the creaking door and the deep voice, our imaginations created images of evil. For some, nightmares resulted from being exposed to these chilling "mystery stories" or sounds. By the hearing of the ear, faith can come, but so can undesirable entities such as fear. A spirit of cursing can be acquired by hearing foul language in the home, and then allowing it to gain a foothold by repeating the same words.

Touch Gate – Parents naturally discourage scratching or rubbing of the genital area to avoid either stimulation, or the formation of an undesirable habit. The child and later adult must learn that there are certain parts of the bodies of others which should not be touched. Children should be warned against allowing others to touch them inappropriately.

Mouth Gate – Tasting things not to be tasted, and drinking or eating to excess are ways that demons may enter through the mouth gate. Spirits also can enter as a result of what comes out of the mouth. When one vocalizes or chooses to give expression to words of lust, profanity or blasphemy, he or she can become vulnerable.

Nose Gate – Smelling or inhaling things one ought not to is an act of willful disobedience and can open a door to addiction. Some of the most heartbreaking addictions which we have encountered have been addictions to the sniffing of substances such as car engine cleaning products, glue and other chemicals. These are in addition to the obvious addictions to illegal substances such as cocaine.

Gate of the Mind – Although not actually a sense gate, the mind is still an avenue utilized by the enemy to gain entry in both children and adults. An undisciplined, or unoccupied mind can invite wrongful thoughts. Thoughts of lust or fear may enter a mind that is either undisciplined or allowed to remain inactive. In older individuals, this is a reason for avoiding a state of "passive mind," or for avoiding such eastern religious practices as "emptying the mind," or "blanking the mind," as well as hypnotism. These types of exercises are an invitation to any demon to take advantage of an open door, or an "empty house." So too are willful disobedience, or the intentional entertaining of wrongful thoughts. As Jesus made clear, the sins of the body are manifested in the mind first...

> But I say unto you, That whosoever looketh on a woman to lust after her hath committed adultery with her already in his heart.
>
> MATT. 5:28

2.

Gate of Heredity

The second gate to consider is the ancestral or hereditary gate. We are well familiar with the physical kinds of problems and sicknesses which pass themselves down family lines. What we are less familiar with are the spiritual traits or sicknesses that also work their way through a family's lineage.

One category of hereditary problems arises from *familiar spirits* or *curses*. We normally consider inheritance to include only those conditions overtly and consistently manifested in the mother, father, grandparents or ancestors. In general, and from a spiritual standpoint, the doors that give legal right of entry to a demon may have been opened a generation or two earlier.

Thus, there are two main routes by which an evil spirit can gain entry to a child, or an unborn fetus. First, and most common, is the root of inheritance. Second, and less common, is through trauma or extreme fear experienced by the mother — as later described in the section on adoption.

The concept of an infant being demonized is particularly offensive to us, because it is especially unfair for an innocent, defenseless child to be vulnerable to demonic invasion. It is, unfortunately, in line with the character of Satan. He is an opportunistic enemy, and is not below mounting an attack upon the weakest and most defenseless among us, including an unborn child.

In most cases, the demonic attack on an infant's personality or well-being *is not* based on the actions of parents. Only in extreme cases, where neglect is involved, does it become, perhaps, more understandable how unborn infants and young toddlers can be targeted. As an example of such an extreme case, drug-addicted parents give birth to drug-addicted babies. This is not unfair on the part of God; it is simply an outworking of the law of cause and effect — self-destructive behavior can affect other people as well. Similarly, the prospective parent who goes to a séance while pregnant, can be exposing the unborn child to Satanic influences and contagion. This can hold true even for a child *not yet conceived.*

Curses tend to work their way through a family's bloodline, and behind every curse is a demon at work. If a great-grandmother, for example, practiced witchcraft, we may see the results of her sin of being involved in "spiritual adultery" manifested in her offspring to the fourth generation (see EXODUS 20:5).

TEMPER TANTRUMS AND STUBBORNNESS

Once by revelation, we learned that stubbornness can be inherited. More specifically, we learned that the root cause precipitating temper tantrums was not always anger, as might be suspected, but rather *stubbornness.* In some cases, extreme stubbornness also exists in a parent or grandparent. The root of repetitive temper tantrums can be, in some cases, the inability to let go of a disappointment, or an attempt to get one's way.

In my own experience, my mother was able to redirect my persistent tantrums by putting cold water on my face.

Children who grow up without being freed from this spirit of stubbornness can find that they are unable to loose themselves from the heaviness and pain that accompanies an emotional hurt such as a rejection or slight. Some may remain in this kind of "tailspin" for days, a full week, or even longer. Spirits that often accompany stubbornness are *perfectionism, melancholy* and *depression.*

HEREDITARY PHYSICAL DISCOMFORT

A personal experience with the hereditary nature of demonic activity occurred when I discovered an inherited spirit of colic. This discovery is described in our book *Power for Deliverance.* Colic can be a manifestation of a physical problem, or it can be the manifestation of a spirit. If it is of a spiritual nature, and not cast out, the latent spirit can open the door for stomach problems or digestive disorders later in life, such as spastic colon, diverticulitis or ulcers.

I experienced my own deliverance from colic, as an adult. Apparently I was a colicky baby, so colic dated back to my infancy. During my deliverance, I had the sensation of a match being lit in my stomach and then passing up my throat and out my mouth. It was extraordinary, to say the least.

There can be parallel ministries that take place between deliverance from a spirit and the healing of a physical condition. Certainly, not all physical ailments are demonic, but Jesus' ministry in the Bible teaches us that some are. In some cases, diabetes runs through the blood lines of families. So too does hypoglycemia. Hypoglycemia is basically the opposite of diabetes and is characterized by low blood sugar and a lack of energy. It, like diabetes, seems to torment families down through the generations. These conditions are not always demonic. But if a spirit is involved, then it can be cast out.

We have ministered to one such family. John, the grown son, came for prayer to be healed of his hypoglycemia. Prayer for healing was offered, and also for deliverance. We bound any spirit related to this condition, cast it out, and broke the hold it had on his life. John was totally healed! However, it took his mother a full year before she could conclude that her son's experience was real, and then came herself for a healing of the same condition. At the time of this writing, their healing has lasted over 15 years!

A few years later, a different couple (Peter and his wife Evelyn) learned that one of their daughters had hypoglycemia, and they also cast it out. This particular family had experienced a *spirit of hypoglycemia* for three generations! They had become familiar with spiritual warfare, and learned how to cast out spirits in the name of Jesus. The result was a breakthrough in a generational affliction, and their daughter's healing soon followed.

All this is to say that a physical condition in one person may be purely physical, but in another it may have a spiritual root. It is always good to pray for both healing and deliverance whenever the opportunity arises.

HEREDITARY MANIPULATION
CAN BEGIN AS EARLY AS THE CRIB

A young mother came to one of my wife's prayer meetings and said she wanted prayer for her attitude toward her six month old daughter who was driving her to distraction. She explained, "Joyce will not let me out of her sight. If I leave the room she immediately starts screaming."

A revelation came forth that the problem was manipulation, and Sue asked the young mother, "Is your own mother manipulative?"

She replied, "Oh boy, is she!"

At the close of the meeting, and without the child being present, the group prayed against the *spirit of witchcraft* in operation in the child, and broke its manipulative hold upon the lineage. We received word soon after that the child experienced an instant change in behavior. No longer restless, she became very peaceful. The witchcraft in this family had skipped a generation, passing from the grandmother to the grandchild, which is not uncommon.

The third gate occurs in growing families...

3.
GATE OF SIBLING RIVALRY

It often comes as a shock to a child to learn that his parents are going to have another child. This is especially true for a first child or for a child who has been the "baby" of the family for a prolonged period. The rationale of the unprepared child, when a new baby comes on the scene, may be:

- "Why do they need another baby, am I not good enough?" (*insecurity*)

- "Maybe they don't love me any more?" (rejection)

- "Maybe they're not satisfied with me and are going to give me away?" (fear of abandonment)

- "Why should a new baby get all the attention I used to get?" (*jealousy*)

A key to avoiding such problems is to prepare the child in advance, by reassuring him or her of their importance to the family, that the child is still greatly loved, and that he or she is getting a friend and playmate, when the baby gets older.

Sibling rivalry is a term used in psychology to describe the competitive problems between children within the same family. Competition may exist for the parents' attention or approval, and may spill over into other areas such as school, sports, and social activities.

The key to solving such rivalries is communication and reinforcement: to assure each child that he or she is accepted and loved by the parents equally, and that each child is important to the family. Encouraging the children to share toys and play together at an early age is helpful, especially if they are close in age, as well as treating each child the same, in so far as possible.

PROBLEMS CONFRONTED IN FAMILIES DEALING WITH DIVORCE OR DEATH

There are certain aspects of sibling rivalry and sibling jealousy that are peculiar to families that have experienced death or divorce. There can arise more deeply rooted problems in single parent homes and also in second family homes.

Step-brothers and step-sisters can present all the same characteristics of rivalry mentioned above, plus the ripe tendency for more jealousy and rejection because of the split loyalties ("He's my father!" or "She's your mother!").

A unique type of rejection often experienced by the child of divorce is when the newly married parents have a new baby. A child in such a situation can react by feeling threatened.

There are at least four possible categories of step-families that can lead (in some cases) to an insecure child:

1. A father or mother dies; and the surviving parent marries and has additional offspring.

2. A mother after a divorce remarries and has offspring. Most frequently children remain with the mother, and therefore, the new baby is born into the household. Fortunately, this allows a pre-birth period of adjustment or mental preparation during the pregnancy for the child to accept the fact of the coming addition.

3. An absent father, who may be in varying degrees of absenteeism or invisibility to the child, begins a new family. Keep in mind, this is often more of a shock to the child, as he or she has not been made aware of (or shielded from) the father's ongoing actions in life.

    Thus the new baby is perceived by the child as a rival and as competition for the little remaining time the father has for his children. It poses a threat to whatever remains of the son-father or daughter-father relationship that has already come under great strain because of the absence of the father. Deep hurts can result and jealousy can enter.

4. When a stepchild is conceived illegitimately, even deeper hurts may occur. Shame, embarrassment and other hurts are added to the ones normally incurred.

Another facet of sibling-rivalry that is less common, but occasionally uncovered, is *sibling hatred*. One child literally hates his brother or sister. Sometimes, the older child resents the appearance of a new addition to the family who threatens the older's role as either the "prince" or "princess" of the home. Or, a younger child may hate the older sibling for abusive treatment when he or she was too little to defend themselves. The hatred can be very real and may last into adulthood. We have encountered extreme cases in which the older sibling has either assisted or stood silently by while the younger has attempted suicide. The solution for this category of sibling rivalry may require deliverance.

4.
GATE OF CHILDHOOD TRAUMA

Traumatic experiences in early life, occurring any time within the vulnerable period of childhood, can provide the door for the opportunistic spiritual enemy to gain entry. This includes even the nine months spent in the womb.

The child can receive a wound in the personality (i.e. soul) through:

- a harmful action of someone else, either intentional or unintentional

- unpleasant or cruel circumstances beyond the child's control.

TRAUMA AT BIRTH

The child's need for deliverance may be the result of accidents or trauma associated with the birthing process. Some birthing traumas involve the loss of the mother as a result of a difficult birth, while other birthing traumas can cause ongoing physical issues of impairment or crippling.

These circumstances are in no way related to, and in no way the result of, any shortcomings on behalf of the parents. Such tragedies occur irrespective of the merit of the individuals, and are not to be interpreted as punishment. Importantly, Scripture teaches:

"Or those eighteen, upon whom the tower in Siloam fell, and slew them, think ye that they were sinners above all men that dwelt in Jerusalem? I tell you, Nay..."   LUKE 13:2–4

"And as Jesus passed by, he saw a man which was blind from his birth. And his disciples asked him, saying, Master, who did sin, this man, or his parents, that he was born blind?
Jesus answered, Neither hath this man sinned, nor his parents..."   JOHN 9:1–3

We observe, in the words of the Master Himself, that accidents do occur, and no relation is made to the victim having brought the tragedy by sinning (e.g. Tower of Siloam). Also, we note the universality of Jesus' ministry to those who were wounded or oppressed: Jesus met the need of every person who came to Him seeking healing (or deliverance). He turned *no one away*, whether because of the quantity or quality of their issues, or even their sins. None were outside of the reach of His earthly ministry of love.

These truths are especially important as they are faith-building and offer encouragement to those of us seeking either deliverance or healing for a child. In particular, we do not have to merit the blessing of the Lord's ministry, nor do we have to attain sinless perfection in order to be eligible for it. Thanks be to Jesus!

CASE: A TORMENTED BABY

Elise, a good friend of the family, told us that she was blessed to have had an easy first baby, and therefore had a standard by which to measure normal feeding and sleeping schedules. Their second child was not as pliable. While the birth of the second child had been easy, the first week after the birth was one of constant turmoil. The baby did not sleep well nor long. The child would wake within minutes of the parents' bedtime. For instance, the child would wake one night as they were about to retire at eight o'clock, and another night as they were about retire at eleven o'clock.

After assuring themselves through their doctor that their baby was not suffering physically, they determined to treat the problem as potentially a spiritual one.

The baby had been born with her eyes and eyelids very bruised. They realized that the fretting might be an indication of spirits that had entered in the trauma of the birth process, as indicated by the bruising.

Elise and her husband determined to pray for their child's deliverance every night, especially against the *spirit of trauma*, when the child awoke prematurely or with painful cries. They did not have long to wait. Each night, for five nights, they spent fifteen or twenty minutes praying quietly over her. The bruises began disappearing by the morning following their first prayer session! Also, the baby slept soundly from then on. She became a baby as easy to manage as her older sister had been. Elise told me that her second child was spared from sleeplessness through the months to come. She also felt that some of Satan's future plans for that child were canceled through their nighttime prayers.

All this, I realize, is pretty heavy teaching in light of what we have been led to believe about babies and their schedules, and about children and their moods. However, we have encountered cases where an infant manifests undue or constant fretting, unhappiness, or irregular schedules, and this was resolved through deliverance from the effects of birthing trauma.

The following account sheds more light on this, and first appeared in the book *Power for Deliverance*.[1] The story is illustrative of a number of points:

> ➤ how *early* a spirit can gain a foothold in a life,

> ➤ how an *innocent infant* can become a victim, and

> ➤ how *long* the effect of a stronghold may remain.

---

1 *Power for Deliverance (Songs of Deliverance)* by Bill Banks, Impact Christian Books, Inc.
  www.impactchristianbooks.com/banks

CASE: DELIVERANCE FOR SALLY FROM "IT"

Sally, a young nurse from our fellowship, phoned one day to ask if my wife and I would pray with her.

"I know that I need further deliverance. I don't have any idea what it is I'm up against, but I'm sure it isn't rejection because we've already dealt with that and I really believe that is gone. This is something related to rejection," she told us. "I know that I'm saved and that the Lord loves me, and that I've been baptized in the Spirit and walking with Him for over five years, but there is still something tormenting me."

I reflected upon the previous ministry with Sally. She had been adopted when only a few days old by an older couple who had lovingly raised her. Having been raised in a home as an only child by older parents and knowing that she had been adopted, Sally had battled rejection and abandonment problems. She had been delivered of both spirits about six months earlier and had also forgiven her birth-mother for abandoning her.

She continued: "It's embarrassing to talk about, but I'm sure most girls, or women, think of themselves as female; as a 'she' or a 'her.' For some reason, I always think of myself as an 'it.' I really don't understand why, but that's always been the way that I've thought of myself. I'm almost thirty years old, and all the dates I've had in my life you could count on one hand. I'm not upset about it because I've had no desire to date either."

I recalled that we had always known Sally to be a friendly, outgoing, loving, patient, and compassionate Christian. We had observed that although she was very pleasant and people genuinely liked her, she did not date. In spite of the fact that she had a great personality, Sally seemed to have no desire to date and did not seem, upon reflection, to be particularly feminine. She always dressed neatly but not in a very feminine way.

We concluded that the torment she experienced behind these feelings could be, in part, demonic. However, we were without any idea as to what she was up against. So I suggested that we pray and ask God to intervene. We prayed a simple prayer, something to this effect:

> "Lord Jesus,
>
> We acknowledge that You are the Deliverer. It is Your ministry and we know that You know all about Sally's life and You want her whole even more than we do. In Your name, we command this thing tormenting her to identify itself and to come out of her."

Then we waited.

Sally began to shake and shiver. It was evident to us that the Lord was doing something, and that she was seeing something in the spiritual realm. Therefore we decided to let the Lord finish His sovereign ministry to her.

A few minutes later she looked up, her eyes wet with tears, and said, "You won't believe what I just saw. I was in a large white room. As I became aware of my surroundings, I was be able to see details in the room. You know I'm a nurse, so I instantly recognized the scene as a hospital delivery room. I could see the clock on the wall. I could see the delivery room staff milling around. I could hear everything they said. I knew everything going on in that room. It was amazing to me. And then I noticed that there was a woman on the table who had just given birth."

Sally paused briefly, and continued: "Suddenly, I felt myself being carried from the corner where I was, out toward the center of the room, and I realized with a start that I was the new-born baby! The nurse carrying me attempted to hand me to the new mother. She took one look at me with a sneer on her face, put up a hand to stop the nurse and snarled, 'Get IT out of here!'"

She sighed deeply and we all then realized that the curse of being an "it" had, in essence, been laid upon her from the moment of her birth. As a result of her being unwanted by her mother and put up for adoption, she had not only acquired the spirits of *rejection* and *abandonment*, but also this unusual and isolating torment that had caused her to think of herself as an "it," a non-female. We then prayed again with her, breaking the curse of being an "it" and casting out the spirit which made her think of herself as not fully female. The results were powerful.

At the close of our session, I asked her if I could pray about her dating situation. She agreed.

As I began to pray, I felt an unusually powerful anointing. I was praying about events completely unknown to me. I began breaking curses that had been placed upon Sally in infancy; I broke the curse of remaining unmarried and having all attempts at love frustrated, a curse that was placed upon her by the wife of the man who had fathered her through her biological mother. I was a little shocked at all the specifics that were coming out of my prayer, things of which I was previously unaware.

Even though I had felt a strong anointing, I wasn't prepared for the next statement that Sally made, "I didn't tell you this before; I forgot to. But God showed me yesterday that the reason that I had been unable to find a man and unable to marry was because a curse had been placed upon me in connection with my father." Her revelation the day before confirmed what the Holy Spirit was suggesting as we ministered the following day!

God is so good and He is so desirous that His people be set free. When they desire to be delivered and take the step to call upon Him, miracles can happen.

Revelations

- AN INDIVIDUAL CAN RECEIVE A SPIRIT FROM THE MOMENT OF BIRTH.

- A SPIRIT ACQUIRED IN CHILDHOOD OR INFANCY CAN HAVE A SERIOUS EFFECT ON THE LIFE OF A CHRISTIAN, EVEN A SPIRIT-BAPTISED BELIEVER.

- SOMETIMES THERE ARE INDICATIONS IN THE PERSONALITY OR LIFE-STYLE OF THE INDIVIDUAL THAT GIVE CLUES AS TO THE SPIRITS INVOLVED.

TRAUMA FROM BEFORE BIRTH (e.g. THE WOMB)

Sally's story is an example of how early in life demonic bondages can enter, including from the moment of birth. To go a step further, in certain cases a spirit can gain entry even before birth. This is a difficult concept, and seems totally unfair to us. Before looking at two ways in which it can happen, let us first consider a Scriptural example. The Bible records that John the Baptist, whose age was birth minus three months and who was thus in the womb of his mother, was filled with the Holy Spirit. If a child in the womb has a capacity to receive the Holy Spirit, then it is also possible that a child in the womb has a capacity to receive an evil spirit.

TRAUMA IN EARLY CHILDHOOD

Many spirits enter the lives of individuals when they were infants or children. Of course, adults can acquire demonic issues later in life, but children, I believe, are the most vulnerable. Their consciousness is developing along with their minds, wills and their awareness of right and wrong.

The young child is vulnerable to many fears because he or she does not yet have the natural defensive weapon of a fully developed mind, the means by which an older individual may rationally defend himself. A child, for instance, who is told that the bogeyman will "get him" may pick up a fear because he is unaware that there is no such being, and that the person who mentioned the bogeyman was only joking.

An incident that occurred when I was about twelve illustrates this truth. My parents were taking my five-year-old brother, his good friend, my sister and I on an afternoon outing to visit a commercially developed cave. The five year old friend of my brother, leaned over the front seat and asked, "Where are we going?"

My Dad, who loved to tease and knowing we had not been outside of the Midwest much, said "Well, we're going to Mexico."

My family all laughed, thinking it was a great joke. But we noticed a few moments later that the guest was sobbing quietly in the back seat with tears running down his cheeks. In spite of a good time at the caverns, and an atoning treat of ice cream cones, our guest didn't really relax until we returned him to his parents.

This had an impact on me. Even totally innocent teasing, or joking, can cause problems for children who, because of their immaturity, have difficulty distinguishing between reality and unreality, truth and fiction. Thus, parents should be careful of joking or teasing with their children, and make sure that the child knows what is a joke.

Trauma Through Death or Sickness

There can be grief and fear experienced by a child when a parent becomes unavailable, including through sickness, being in prison, being in a sanitarium, or spending lengths of time in a hospital.

In particular, it is very difficult for a child to grasp the concept of death. Death can be traumatic in the loss of a loved one, or a pet. But even the death of someone they did not know well can be quite traumatic.

Case: Death of a Parent

We encountered a demonic doorway from a fear of death in our own family. I was a terminal cancer patient in 1970 when my oldest son, Kevin, was about three and a half. I was hospitalized for several months, prior to being healed sovereignly and miraculously by the Lord. Kevin visited me at the hospital before I came home, and was very loving and affectionate. The day I returned home, he gave me a good hug, a "big love," and said "Hi Dad, sure glad you're home. Glad to see you," and went out to play.

We thought my younger son, Stephen (at one-and-a-half), hadn't been old enough to grasp the gravity of the situation. When I returned home, however, he crawled up into my lap. He put his arms around my neck, and hung on for all he was worth for at least forty-five minutes, which a returning father didn't mind at all. However, it did show us that my illness and absence from the home had made a far greater impression on his little mind or spirit than we had imagined.

We made the assumption that Kevin had taken it in stride. However, when he was about eleven, we noticed a change in his personality. All of a sudden, he was no longer able to receive affection from me. He would get very giddy and silly when I was around him. I first noticed it manifesting one night when I went into the boys' bedroom to say prayers with them. He wouldn't let me kiss him goodnight.

He could receive affection from his mother and other relatives, and he was loving toward me at other times. But at night, when I prayed with him and tried to kiss him before bed, he was not able to receive it.

It was peculiar. We thought it might be symptomatic of something deeper, although we weren't sure just what. Since we were not able to resolve this behavior any other way, we decided to try a natural approach of having me spend extra time alone with him. I set aside a half hour every evening to spend with just him, playing ping-pong, cards, or whatever he wanted to do. I just wanted to have some quality time with him.

After about two or three months, one night when I went in to say prayers with him, he prayed a prayer that caused my jaw to drop, tears to fill my eyes, and a light of understanding to dawn. His prayer went something like this, "Dear Jesus, thank you for not letting my Daddy die."

Here, once again, our assumptions had been incorrect. There had been a wound to his spirit due to my absence and illness, a wound greater than we could have imagined. Because of this wound to his spirit, a fear had entered. It was an unspeakable fear, so deep that he had been unable to articulate it. It was the fear that he would lose his father through death. After he prayed that short prayer that night, he was set free from this lingering torment. From that time on he was able to both receive and give normal, healthy affection toward me. The power of love and trust had broken the barrier of fear. God's light was brought to shine on this area of darkness. It had brought deliverance.

CASE: KATHY & THE DEATH OF A RELATIVE

Kathy, a beautiful young girl came to visit me one afternoon and said, "My problem is kind of strange. I have dated very few times in my life, although I am 27. I get extremely nervous before I go on a date." She continued, "I agree to go out with someone, and then I hate the thought of going and even become physically ill." She concluded, "I don't think that's natural."

I agreed, it did not seem natural. She had at one point even attempted suicide because she felt so abnormal. Her sisters had all dated normally, and were in fact all married, as was her brother. Her sisters and brother, as siblings often do, urged her to date which added to the pressure she already felt.

She had prefaced our conversation by saying, "I do want to get married: I want to have a normal life. My goal is to be married and have children, but I just absolutely panic at the thought of a date."

We spent half an hour searching for any hint of a problem from her past, including rejection, or molestation in childhood, or any variation of being mistreated by a member of the opposite sex. We found nothing to speak of. No one in her family had experienced divorce. We were at a loss in our search for a root. She did not have any problem being around men whom she did not consider a potential date. "I get along fine with all the men at work," she noted.

The only intriguing thought that had surfaced was that she had a fear of broken relationships. This did not seem to make any sense based on her history. She could not explain it. Her parents were happily married; her relatives were all happily married.

As we waited on the Lord, she was suddenly reminded of an uncle: "Well something came to my mind as we've been talking. I don't understand what it has to do with any of this. But," she said, "I remember when I was a child of five or six, my aunt came to our house and told my mother about the death of their brother, my uncle, who had been killed in the war." Tears came into her eyes. It was obvious that Kathy had been deeply hurt and that a fear of some kind had entered at this point in her childhood related to the death of this relative.

I asked if she had known him fairly well, and she said "Yes, although I was too young to have identified with him as anything other than a relative." It came to the surface during our prayer time that the fear of losing a loved one had been the root of the anxiety in her personal life. Kathy had been frightened, as a little child, by seeing and experiencing the hurt that her mother suffered over the loss of Kathy's uncle.

It can be an extremely traumatic experience for children to witness the shock, pain, and hurt of a parent learning about the death of a loved one. I recall, as a child myself, that the only time I ever saw my father cry was when he learned of the death of his mother. I was probably about eleven at the time, and it made a deep impression on me, because it was the only time I'd ever seen tears in his eyes. I remember trying to comfort him, feeling a little stupid afterwards about what I'd said. The only comfort I could offer him, from my limited experience, was to tell him I had felt the same way the year before when my dog had been hit by a car.

As a child, I was unable to fully grasp the gravity of death but somehow the weight of this experience lingered inside me into my adult life.

Revelations

• A YOUNG CHILD IS VULNERABLE TO MANY FEARS BECAUSE HE DOES NOT HAVE THE NATURAL DEFENSIVE WEAPON OF A FULLY DEVELOPED MIND.

• A SPIRIT CAN ENTER A CHILD WHEN OBSERVING GRIEF, FEAR OR HURT BY A LOVED ONE

CASE: MAISIE & THE FEAR OF DEATH

Maisie, a young mother, came seeking deliverance after reading *Power for Deliverance*. Her story was unique in that it contained more fears regarding death than I had ever encountered before, or since. The fear of death was extremely real to Maisie; she slept at night with the light on and her head under the covers. She said she felt each night that she might die before morning.

Maisie had accumulated a dozen different versions of the fear of death over the course of her life. These tormenting spirits had entered her as a result of:

1. She was *rejected* by her father before birth. He didn't want another child, and tried to talk her mother into having an abortion. This was the first doorway of entry for the spirit of the fear of death.

2. Her mother became so depressed by his attitude that she seriously contemplated *suicide*, a spirit that was passed on to Maisie.

3. Maisie was born prematurely. The doctor mistakenly gave her mother an injection of a labor inducing drug, and Maisie *nearly died* shortly after birth.

4. Her father divorced her mother when she was about three, and a *fear of abandonment* entered.

5. Maisie experienced the *death of her care-provider*, an aunt who had taken her in while her mother worked to provide income. The aunt died when Maisie was five, compounding the fear of death already present.

6. Her grandmother had *died of a heart attack*, and now Maisie feared exercise in all forms. This fear prevented her taking off the weight she wanted to lose, and added strain on her own marriage.

7. She acquired a fear of bleeding to death. This *fear of hemorrhaging* entered her when her menstrual cycle started without her having had any preparation or explanation whatsoever.

8. She had a fear of the *death of a parent*. This spirit was similar to the fear of abandonment, but had entered her when she was a teenager when she had been emotionally isolated and alone.

9. Fear related to *committing fornication.* This led to a fear of death in the form of punishment, and she would became short of breath.

10. A fear of *terminal illness* was also present. She had a gland that was swollen in her neck and had became convinced that she had cancer and feared dying of that disease.

11. Fear of *other physical ailments.* She developed a condition diagnosed as asthma, which led her to believe she was again terminally ill.

12. She began having *anxiety attacks* each time that she became short of breath. Dizziness resulted with the spirits telling her she was going to die.

Maisie had the longest chain of *death spirits* that I can ever recall encountering. However, several of Maisie's torments are fairly common sources for demonic oppression to enter a child: premature birth or birth trauma, death of a parent or care-giver, guilt over sin, and fears related to physical ailments.

We rebuked each death-related spirit and cast them out of Maisie, and as time went by, she was beautifully set free.

TRAUMA DURING PUBERTY

Trauma can also occur during puberty. This time in a person's life can sometimes create a root of fear, as the following case illustrates.

CASE: GLENDA'S STORY

Glenda's problems stemmed from accidents and trauma. She came for ministry as an adult, and was in the process of raising several teen-aged children of her own. Glenda began by saying, "I need deliverance. I've read the books you recommended, and have brought a list of the strongholds I feel I need to have broken."

In an orderly fashion, we dealt with each spirit by naming it, and then commanding it to leave. *Claustrophobia* was on her list, and she said bluntly, "I don't know why I have it; to my knowledge I've never been confined in a tight place or anything similar, but I really am claustrophobic. Any room without windows or even an elevator bothers me."

We began to pray specifically about this fear of enclosed places, when she suddenly exclaimed, "Oh! I think the Lord just reminded me of something. I just saw myself locked in a small, dark closet under our basement stairs, in the house where I lived as a child. And then I remembered an incident where I panicked. I was crying and screaming, begging my sister to let me out. But she wouldn't."

Glenda paused, wiped away the tears and continued, "I guess that was how it entered." The Lord very graciously revealed to her the source of her claustrophobia.

It is a great help when the Lord enables — or spurs — a person to recall an incident that opened the door to a spirit. Light is brought to bear upon the work of darkness, thus dispelling it. As John states in the first chapter of his Gospel, Light (Jesus) overcomes the darkness. Darkness cannot continue to exist in the presence of light. Evil spirits cannot remain in the presence of the light of Jesus. They fear exposure to the light, and they fear being cast out.

We dealt relatively easily with this spirit of *claustrophobia*, and in agreement, we cast it out of her. Glenda had very little manifestation, other than a few tears.

Then we came to the end of her list of strongholds in her life, and she mentioned one more area. "There is one thing I added to the end of my list of torments; it is probably insignificant, but I mention it anyway. It is a fear of blood."

She could in no way account for her fear of blood. So we began to command the spirit of the *fear of blood* to manifest itself, and to reveal how it entered. Glenda suddenly shuddered and then blushed. "This seems so strange, and it's embarrassing, but I think the Lord just showed how it entered. I saw myself as a little girl of about eleven and a half, or twelve, lying in the old brass bed I slept in as a child. I was hanging onto the brass rails on the headboard, and crying violently. I was afraid that I was dying."

"Why did you think you were dying?" I asked.

"Because my menstrual period had just started for the first time; and I thought I was hemorrhaging and was going to bleed to death! No one had ever explained anything about this to me. My mother didn't have a very good relationship with any of her kids, and probably didn't feel comfortable discussing periods. She probably figured nature would take its course."

We then, in agreement, cast out the spirit of the *fear of blood* and its root *fear of bleeding to death*, both of which entered at the beginning of her menstrual cycle. Glenda later reported being totally free of this long-time fear related to blood.

Revelations

- SPIRITS CAN ENTER A CHILD AS THE RESULT OF AN ACCIDENT OR SOMEONE ELSE'S SIN OR NEGLECT.

- THE INCEPTION OF MENSTRUATION CAN BE VERY TRAUMATIC FOR A YOUNG GIRL AND THE FEAR INVOLVED CAN OPEN HER TO DEMONIC OPPRESSION.

TRAUMA AT SCHOOL

School-aged children can have numerous insecurities: fear of tests, fear of giving reports, fear of a new school, fear of new teachers, fear of new classmates, peer pressure, and so on. Each of these, if discerned, should be confronted, and explained as being normal but harmful. If the child is not freed from these fears through explanation, discussion and prayer, then a *spirit of fear* may be present and need to be cast out.

The teacher, who labels a student as slow, ineducable, or unable to grasp a specific subject such as math, may affect the child in more ways than one, and possibly for the rest of his or her life. If the school system accepts the teacher's evaluation, it is a matter of record — whether true or not. Furthermore, if the teacher tells the student that he or she "will never grasp math," the teacher is imposing a conclusion on the child, who has no reason not to believe the bad report of an authority figure. Thus, the child lives with a stigma, a self-doubt in this area of learning. This may, for instance, lead the child to choose courses throughout his or her school years to avoid a specific subject, like math. In essence, the teacher's statement becomes a self-fulfilling prophecy.

On the opposite side of the spectrum, a child who is always placed in advanced classes, and due to grading on the curve is never able to make good grades, may erroneously believe himself or herself to be a poor achiever.

TRAUMA AS REVEALED IN DREAMS

Dreams can influence children for good or for bad. In the Bible, for instance, Joseph's dreams as a child were prophetic. However, if a child has reoccurring dreams of a frightening nature, there is a possibility that something spiritual may be going on.

If a child dreams repetitively that he or she has lost a parent (or both parents), or that he or she is lost and cannot find home, or that he or she is abandoned and left alone, then there is the possibility that demonic activity is taking place. When a child has a bad dream, the parent should pray with him or her for protection against any fears that may have resulted from the dream. A rule of thumb is that anything that causes torment has some form of demonic initiative. It is always a good idea, whenever possible, to say prayers over a child as they go to bed, for their sleep to be blessed.

If there is a particular recurrent fear in dreams, then the parent should attempt to analyze it for its source. If, for example, the child is repeatedly dreaming about being beaten up on the way to school, talk with him or her and try to determine if there is a basis in fact for the fear. It may be that a bully has been threatening the child. Parents should not pass off those dreams and fears as unreal, but make themselves an *ally with their child* and teach the child to confront those fears. We try to repeat the fact, with children and adults, that the devil is first and foremost a liar (JOHN 8:44B).

Some psychologists consider dreams to be doorways into the unconscious mind. Considering the vulnerability of children, bad dreams, nightmares, or even occult dreams can be manifestations of the activity of demons — or indications that demons are *attempting to gain entry*.

A good friend and fellow deliverance minister once asked for deliverance for himself. He said, "I know this fear seems kind of silly. But it's a real, tormenting type of fear that hits me frequently in nightmares. I see a monster-type of figure and the closest way I can describe it would be to say it looks like the abominable snowman. I began seeing this thing in my dreams when I was in grade school."

He could not recall how the "thing" had entered, so we simply agreed and cast it out by its characteristics. "You, spirit that manifests as an abominable snowman, come out of him in Jesus' name!" Several years later, he happened to share this experience with a good friend, a police officer, who responded, "That's the exact same thing I've had in my dreams!"

Such monster-type creatures who inhabit our nightmares, or

make frequent appearances in them, commonly enter as a result of movies, books, or other media that is intended to shock and instill fear. Recently, I received a phone call from a man who wanted to be delivered of a "sea monster" creature that had been tormenting him in his dreams. He explained, "I know I picked this thing up when I saw a monster movie as a kid." Because he already knew the source of his problem, we prayed for his deliverance over the phone.

Logical, or illogical, fears are often common ways that demons can affect childhood. A fear of falling, for example, or a fear of being pushed off a ledge, can be very logical. If someone had teased you by threatening to push you off a ledge or from a high place, you could have received through this traumatic experience a *fear of heights* or a *fear of falling*. Similarly, someone dunking you under water, or threatening to drown you during play in a pool, can give entry for the *fear of drowning, fear of water, fear of suffocation*, or a *fear of death*. While such behavior was intended as play, such a brief encounter with terror in a child's life can have lasting effects.

5.
GATE OF ABUSE

The parent who abuses his child physically, verbally, or sexually leaves the child with a gaping wound in the soul — a crack in the personality — and it remains festering until it receives God's prescribed remedy. Try as he or she might, the child (or adult) cannot erase the feelings of hurt, grief or pain. It may take years before the victim comes to the point of being able to call the abuse for what it was, and thus distinguish between normal behavior and abuse. It could take years before the victim is willing to face the past, forgive the abuser and receive deliverance.

I was approached by the grandparents of two children who were being abused by their drug-addicted parents. Since a court date had been set, I asked a good friend, who is a social worker in that city, if she could help us get the children into protective custody. I gave her the full names of the boy and girl, and I was shocked when she replied, "I'll need more information, such as dates of birth, parents' full names and mother's maiden name."

"Why do you need all that information to find an abused boy and girl whose names I have already given you?" I asked.

She replied, "I have five pages of that same last name. We have over ten thousand active cases of child abuse in this city alone."

I reeled mentally at that figure, considering that the city she was referring to had a population of about 400,000, and that does not include the surrounding suburban areas.

The social worker linked the abuse of children to drugs. She continued, "It has become so bad that I no longer ask if drugs are involved in child abuse cases, I just ask them *which drugs they're doing.*"

Drugs do play a large part in child abuse, a fact that often goes unmentioned. Modern man has scoffed at the idea that spiritual doorways can be opened through drug use. There is a sense of pride in refusing to believe that something stronger or more intelligent can enter while in the altered state of produced through drugs.

The effects of abortion, and the attitude of our nation toward it, also plays a role in the epidemic of child abuse. When a woman (and/or birth father) makes the decision to murder a child in the womb, the murderous hate often remains beneath the surface in the individual, as a demonic stronghold inside, and will affect his or her relationship with future children until it is confronted and cast out. That is, even though the parent means no harm to their child, the child may sense the spirit from the prior abortion (see the GATE OF ABANDONMENT later in this chapter for more information).

There are many parallels between physical wounds in our flesh and spiritual wounds to our souls. Forgiveness to the soul is like antiseptic to a cut or wound. When a wound is fresh, deliverance may not be required. If a person is engaged with Jesus directly, or through a pastor or counselor, the infection of demons can be avoided. If, for example, the victim forgives the one who has committed the wrong speedily, not allowing "the sun to go down upon your wrath," then he or she will not give "Satan any place" within their soul (EPH. 4:26–27). This will most likely prevent demonic entry. Again, forgiveness to the soul is like antiseptic to a cut or wound.

If a proactive attitude is taken shortly after the wrong is incurred, the demon has not gained a stronghold, or is fairly easy to dislodge. This is a good argument for ministering forgiveness and deliverance to children, to spare them from torments that can linger through adulthood. If we were raised in homes with parents who never considered demons a reality, our parents may still have practiced a basic form of deliverance on us when they taught us, and insisted, that we forgive the people who wronged us.

VERBAL ABUSE

Particularly vicious to a child's soul is verbal abuse. Although it comes forth from the mouth, it reflects an attitude of the heart, and the child senses the hate which motivates the unkind words. It can be as damaging to the soul of a child as physical abuse is to the body. The old adage "sticks and stones may break my bones, but words can never hurt me" is a lie. Words hurt far worse than do blows or even broken bones, as the bones may heal and be forgotten within a few months. But the sting and hurt of unkind words can haunt an individual throughout his or her lifetime.

The practice of teasing one another, ridiculing, and name calling in childhood — seemingly innocent — can get out-of-hand and become abusive. As children, we tend to be extremely susceptible to Satan's lies, and often fall prey to either believing or being hurt by unjust labels.

I recall a situation, when I was in the early years of grade school, involving a nice girl in our class named Carla. Someone, probably a boy who liked her but who didn't know how to express his attraction at that early age, began to tease her. It was said, and the word spread, that she had "cooties." What began as an innocent game of avoiding contact with this girl soon got out of hand.

The teacher finally had to admonish the class for our cruelty towards the girl. I recall that I felt terrible for being involved in it, even if only to the extent of silently allowing the teasing that went on. I too fell prey to the game when I noticed a small scar on my wrist, that I didn't recall having before. It was on the exact spot where Carla had touched my wrist. Even though I recognize today the foolishness of that idea, for sometime I believed — at least partially — that the scar was a result of her having touched me. I always liked Carla and later, when I was in college, she dated one of my friends. But to this day, when I see that scar, I think of it as the misnamed "Carla's scar" and recall with remorse the mistreatment she received by our class.

From the vantage point of a mature mind, we find it difficult to conceive that a child could seriously believe something that is so foolish. But, as we have learned through the deliverance ministry, they can. I would later learn the hard way with one of my own boys.

We encountered an unusual fear in one of my sons. He said he couldn't explain it exactly, but he had a series of nightmares in which he felt that he was trapped in a field of pipes. The picture he saw in his dreams looked like a big plant, like a gasoline or oil refining plant with large pipes sticking up. The Lord then impressed on us that this was a fear that began when he was a small child.

In fact, the Holy Spirit pointed to a specific time in his life, around the age of three. I remembered that he would come into the bathroom in the morning and tickle me, or crack me in the leg to distract me while I was shaving. On one occasion, I jokingly picked him up and held him over my shoulder. I told him I was going to "flush him down the toilet."

I remember vividly being amazed at how he went into an absolute state of panic. He became hysterical that morning when I held him in the air. I could not believe he thought that I'd hurt him, and I told him that it was a joke and I did not want to harm him in any way. But the panic was real. I was very sorry to have scared him and asked him that morning to forgive me. When he calmed down, I thought it was long gone.

Now, more than nine years after the incident, the nightmares started to occur. We then realized what had taken hold of him and was manifesting through his nightmares. We were confronted by a tormenting fear that had entered him and was now manifesting itself almost ten years later! We cast it out, and there was no further recurrence.

OVER-DISCIPLINE AS ABUSE

"...fathers, provoke not your children to wrath: but bring them up in the nurture and admonition of the Lord."

EPH. 6:4

Children are by nature loving and forgiving, and can accept far more discipline and punishment from parents than we might expect. There are times, however, when discipline may involve excessive punishment. Many spirits can enter as a result, depending upon the personality of the child. One child may manifest obsessive guilt or inferiority, another hatred, rebellion and even violence.

If your child tells you that he or she has been unfairly treated by an adult, take a moment to realize that this perception may, or may not, be accurate. Sometimes a child resents discipline from an outsider and exaggerates details of the abuse to "get even." Sometimes, parents storm into the child's school to confront the teacher without all the facts, causing the child to believe that lying, and rebellion against authority, can be beneficial. However, if the situation turns out to be of valid concern, then our role as parents — and our duty — is to protect the welfare of our children and that includes the child's *personality* or *soul*.

Keep in mind that no one can be treated fairly at all times. Our sons have had to endure many unfair situations, a few with teachers and some with other students, and have had to learn to manage and forgive. In a few cases, looking back, we know that we failed to step in when we should have, and fears developed as a result. Parenting is not always easy and is often less than perfect.

Through ministry we have heard of numerous examples where parents should have stepped in to protect the heart of a child. One example was abuse of a young boy by a cub-scout master who made the boys "run a gauntlet" of fist blows for minor infractions of rules. In this case, the child should have been (and finally was) removed from the troop and the troop leadership question addressed.

ABUSE THROUGH SEXUAL EXPERIENCES

There are certain sexual sins that aren't possible until after puberty. Puberty opens the child to a whole new arena of possibilities for encounters with sin.

Demons can enter through bad sexual experiences. There was a recent case of a three year old boy who was being regularly molested by his divorced father while on visitation. The mother was unable to get the courts to aid in her attempts to block the ongoing abuse. News headlines have also recently featured a number of cases in which small children, both male and female, were molested by drunken (or drugged) fathers, uncles or neighbors. These experiences leave tremendous scars, and can become doorways for demons of trauma to cause torment.

A woman came to my office and said she wanted a book that would give her more information about demons. She said that although her church and its denomination do not believe in demons, or that Christians can have them, she knew that demons were real. She explained, "I work for the government as a social worker, and deal with cases of sexually abused children. You can't tell me that demons aren't real: even in Christian children." She knew from experience, not theology, the reality of demons.

The deleterious effects of the more obvious and heinous abuse of children in the form of physical or sexual abuse are being recognized today as more and more cases come to light.

However, the enemy can use innocent incidents to open a child to fear and guilt. One young boy, while sleeping one night with his father, realized that the father had become erect. The boy thought he had somehow produced or provoked that reaction in his father, and grew up carrying feelings of guilt, and doubts about his own sexuality.

We have encountered almost the identical situation with young daughters sleeping near their fathers. Because the fathers became erect in their sleep, Satan was able to lie to the girls causing them to believe they were harlots, or to fear that they were pregnant. Their experience left them with extreme guilt, and a fear of men and sex.

Some children are raised under extremely terrible circumstances, in situations that would be difficult for most of us to believe. We had the opportunity to pray for one young girl, who had been in and out of mental institutions. She had been raised by a mother who had turned to prostitution to support herself and her child. One night, one of her customers became unruly. A fight ensued, and the customer, a serviceman, was stabbed and killed. The girl was young, and was so traumatized by the blood, the scene and the screaming, that to this day she does not know whether she or her mother killed the man. The drunken mother apparently told the police that the daughter had stabbed the customer to prevent the mother from being beaten.

Self-doubt about one's sexuality can be forced onto a young person through a traumatic and unwanted sexual encounter. We have seen, for instance, that homosexuality is a *spirit* (see CASE 6 in *Power for Deliverance*). Traumatic encounters with this kind of abuse at an early age can give a foothold to Satan, and aid his attempt to hook his victims as early as possible. These children are not sufficiently mature to resist, and often manipulated by the offender. Some survivors of this kind of abuse can resist a life of wounded sexuality through the love and acceptance and support of the family, and through counseling. This indicates that the end result of becoming sexually promiscuous or homosexual does not automatically occur.

Unfortunately, in many of the cases of sexual abuse, the problem is compounded by the victim's guilt and shame, which creates a fear of telling anyone. This allows Satan to gain a two-fold advantage: 1.) the trauma from the perverted encounter, and 2.) the problem being shrouded in darkness and silence so that no compassion, love, encouragement, or counseling can be ministered. The victim feels unwarranted guilt and shame for being an unwilling victim of the heterosexual or homosexual encounter. Bringing the hidden things out into the light, in whatever manner the Lord leads, can be a major step in the healing process.

There should be no blame placed on a child for the abuse caused by someone else. Satan's intent is to cause the most harm. He intends to isolate a child through fear and shame, and then to condemn the child through guilt and torment. This denies comfort to the innocent victim, while creating a doorway for tormenting spirits to further harm the child's personality.

Pornography in a home creates its own set of problems for children. The initial encounter with pornography is traumatic. The child feels both the stirring within of desires he or she is not able to understand, and at the same time the terror of being exposed for what he or she has seen. The soul of the little child receives a wound. This is another area where love, compassion, good communication, counseling and deliverance can be of great help.

Self-gratification of a sexual nature, or "masturbation," can often occur when a child is exposed to the presence of pornography. Masturbation is an addiction and behind it is a demonic spirit. Children and adults can be set free from this addiction.

The most important roles of a parent are protection and then communication. Depending on the age of the child, a parent sharing with the child his or her own feelings greatly helps in opening avenues for communication and loving ministry. This positive communication lets the child know that he or she is not unusual or odd to have had such feelings, as Satan would have them believe. The child also needs to know that the parent wants to help him or her work through the lust that arose from exposure to pornography, to rid the child of things that make them feel bad about themselves. Lust, it should be noted, is a counterfeit to God's love, which is both pure and holy.

Finally, it should be noted that ritualistic child abuse does occur, even in the most developed of societies. The depravity of satanic ritualistic practices have contributed to the current rash of child abuse in many forms. The child is left with more than physical scars, and feels totally helpless; there may be no one to really care for the child, to add to a sense of worthlessness. There is no one he or she can trust.

Tragically, in certain areas of our country, satanic cult members have attained powerful positions in the legal, justice, and social systems. As a result, protection is afforded to those who engage in these depraved practices and they are released with little or no penalty when caught. In one instance, a warlock charged with more than thirty counts of sexual abuse of children was released and acquitted. In the opinion of the medical examiner, who had examined each of the thirty children, the evidence against the man was incontrovertible and yet he went free.

6.
GATE OF "WRONG" GENDER

A child that is born of the opposite gender than desired can be affected deep in their little soul. This subtle rejection can be from one parent, or both parents. An example is the mother who wanted a son for her husband, and consequently either hates or blames the daughter for being the wrong sex. This mother may dress the girl and treat her as if she was a boy. Some wives and husbands feel they need a male heir to extend the family lineage, or reinforce the masculinity of the father. This dissatisfaction toward the sex of the child, whether expressed outright or internalized, causes confusion as to the child's proper role. Such confusion and frustration can open the door for Satan's deceptions of non-feminine, or non-male spirits, including homosexuality or lesbianism. Sometimes it only takes an off-hand remark such as, "Why couldn't you have been the daughter (e.g. or son) I always wanted," to open a door of wounding. Other times it could be a cruel comment. One instance I am aware of nearly destroyed a girl's life, "If you'd been the son I wanted to give your father, he would have come home alive to us from the war."

CASE: CORA LEFT WITH A FEELING OF NO SELF-WORTH

A refined young lady named Cora came to see us with the complaint that she felt inner turmoil and needed deliverance. "Although I am in my thirties and have children of my own, I am not able to deal with some things in my own life," she said sadly. We sat down privately in the parlor of a church in Tennessee, where I had been invited to conduct a healing service.

Cora began unfolding her story. "I feel like I don't belong anywhere. I feel like I'm a nothing. I am pretty sure this stems from childhood. I could never communicate well with my father."

I had known and respected her father, a popular Pentecostal preacher and pastor, and knew both her parents to be sweet, loving people. Cora's perceptions were, however, somewhat different. She continued, "I was unplanned; or I suspect unwanted… I'm not entirely sure. But I don't think I was what they wanted. My father wanted a son, and I think I was a great disappointment to him, being a girl."

"I grew up as a tomboy, trying to excel in sports, in order to win his approval. I also tried to excel academically at school. I was a top student, but nothing seemed sufficient to get the approval of my father. I never felt I had my father's love and full acceptance. I therefore had great difficulty believing in God's love. In addition, my father was an authority figure — not just for me but for the other members of the church. And since he was always the one who was up front, the church seemed to be his 'show.' It was him, plus God. Our family revolved around the authority of 'the system,' the denomination. Not too surprisingly, I became rebellious against him, and the system, and the hypocrisy that I saw within the denomination's structure."

"My parents were very poor when I was growing up, and I know that I have a *fear of poverty.* I also continually fear *failure.* I think I have a problem with *perfectionism* as well. I fear rejection, and I fear hurt; I was hurt terribly by feeling that my parents didn't really want me. I know that I have *resentment* against my father and against God for allowing all these situations to exist in my life."

Many have been prevented from receiving God's love because of the same kind of problems Cora had. It is difficult for an individual to believe that he or she can have a close relationship with a God who is invisible, when he or she is unable to have one with an earthly father who is visible. Fortunately for Cora, she recognized the source of her problems and confronted them, finding freedom and peace through deliverance.

When a child has experienced rejection related to his or her gender, a deliverance prayer may need to be offered. In such cases, we have seen great value in binding the fear of being the wrong sex, the fear of being homosexual or lesbian, and the fear of being mentally ill.

7.
GATE OF BREAKING FAITH

Wounds to a soul can be caused by breaking faith with a child.

"Yea, mine own familiar friend, in whom I trusted, which did eat
of my bread, hath lifted up his heel against me."

PSA. 41:9

We have found the three most common doorways for spirits to enter children to be:

1. **Not receiving love.** A child does not sense the love of a parent in the way the child's heart expects or desires to receive it.

One hopes to receive love, consideration, and fair treatment from parents. The intertwined spirits of rejection and rebellion usually stem from an experience of feeling unloved or unwanted as a child. The first murder in the Bible resulted from Cain feeling unaccepted, which then, I believe, opened him to spirits of jealousy, hatred and murder.

A subtle form of child neglect is *indifference*. The parent who is not concerned about a child, who does not love the child, has hurt the child deeply without even saying a word.

2. **Being betrayed.** Betrayal, or having one's expectations dashed, especially by a parent, can have lasting effects.

It hurts when you trust someone and that person lets you down. In a parent-child relationship, it can be as simple as canceling a fishing trip or breaking a promise to attend a sporting event. These by themselves do not constitute demonic doorways. But repetitive failures to show up can. Again, a wound may occur to the soul or personality of the child.

We let our guard down around family and friends. When one of them breaks faith with you, through broken promises (such as the marriage covenant, or the implied covenant between parent and child) then a wound occurs. The victim receives a spiritually bleeding, deep internal wound.

> **3.) Suffering loss through death or divorce.** As previously mentioned, when a child loses a parent or someone very close, or there is a divorce, these traumatic experiences can be a gateway for demonic activity.

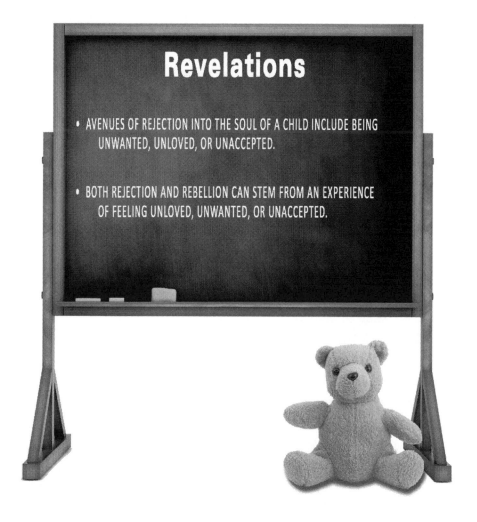

Revelations

- AVENUES OF REJECTION INTO THE SOUL OF A CHILD INCLUDE BEING UNWANTED, UNLOVED, OR UNACCEPTED.

- BOTH REJECTION AND REBELLION CAN STEM FROM AN EXPERIENCE OF FEELING UNLOVED, UNWANTED, OR UNACCEPTED.

8.

GATE OF REJECTION BY LOVED ONES

Rejection is related to the "Gate of Breaking Faith" mentioned in the last section. Due to its prevalence, rejection deserves its own category. It is a familiar gate of torment for adults, and often has its roots from early childhood through the teenage years.

CASE: MELANIE (MEMORIES FROM 13 MONTHS)

Melanie had asked for ministry. She was aware of a spirit of *rejection*, and a spirit of *self-hate*, tormenting her. This all began at the incredibly early age of thirteen months. When she was scarcely more than a year old, she suffered a Grand Mal epileptic seizure, and vividly recalls the looks of shock and distress on her parents' faces as they pulled away from her in horror. To these two early roots of *rejection* and *self-hate*, more than forty additional spirits attached themselves. Melanie was at the brink, being suicidal and barely able to function. She had sought help through counseling, psychology, psychoanalysis and psychiatry, and had achieved momentary relief but no lasting help. She finally became desperate enough to investigate the idea of demonic roots and strongholds, and came to us for deliverance. She was set free.

We have noted that most demonic strongholds are established in childhood, including through the teenage years. We also note that 95% of our deliverance ministry is to born again Christians, and especially spirit-filled Christians — thus putting to rest the question of whether a Christian can have a demonic stronghold in their life. With regard to these Christians who have come to us for deliverance ministry, the vast majority of the demonic strongholds in their lives were acquired before they became born-again. It should also be noted that it is especially rare for Christians to pick up demonic spirits, or have demonic strongholds established, after they have become baptized in the Holy Spirit.

I have, however, seen pastors receive sovereign and striking deliverance from spirits of *hurt* and *rejection* suffered at the hands of members of their congregation. As with children, adults are most deeply and easily hurt by those whom we love, and by those whom we trust. This can include fellow members of the body of Christ.

Why is this so? In part, because we let our spiritual guard down among fellow believers. A heathen can call me a liar, a fool, or crazy to trust God as I do, and it doesn't phase me at all. I expect to be rejected by the world, and I have my spiritual guard up against them. But, when a fellow believer implies that I'm off course spiritually, it can hurt to a devastating effect.

An enemy can call you ugly and it's of no concern. But, if a parent implies you are less than normally attractive, you are crushed. The source can be far more significant than the words actually spoken. As parents, there is a fine walk between correction and rejection, and we need to be aware that a child may perceive things differently than we do. Parents need to be on guard against rejection in their child, while also being firm in their parenting — this is best achieved through dependence on the Holy Spirit, and we highly recommend all Christian parents pursue the *baptism in the Holy Spirit.*

9.
GATE OF VICARIOUS PAIN

The normal pattern of demonic entry for a child is through traumatic experiences. An example would be a bee sting, where a child may pick up a spirit of the *fear of bees*. Similarly, we have encountered people with a *fear of birds* due to experiences in their childhood. We have even ministered to people who feared birds because of movies they had seen.

However, we have observed over time that a child need not have had an actual experience in order to pick up a tormenting spirit related to that experience. This can occur vicariously. A young, impressionable mind can hear about a frightening event, or witness someone else having a frightening event, and pick up the fear too.

We received an interesting illustration of this truth during a healing service. A woman came forward for prayer for chronic, undiagnosed, severe back pain. We ministered healing to her and after the first prayer, she was able to walk about with less pain. "But," she said, "I still have one terribly painful spot." Subsequent prayer did not eliminate the pain, so we asked, "When did this terrible pain first begin?"

Immediately she responded, "I know exactly when it began. I can tell you the very moment. It began while I was talking on the phone with my sister."

"I had called my sister in the hospital to ask about her operation. She was telling me how painful her back surgery had been, and I began to notice a pain in my back as well. Do you think there might be a connection?"

Having learned never to underestimate the outlandish nature of the enemy, we agreed to pray. We cast out the spirit of *back pain* that had entered through hearing of her sister's pain. She was instantly and totally healed, freed of all pain! She left the meeting with a complete healing.

A similar case involved an active, athletic boy whose older sister was seriously injured when struck by an automobile. This accident resulted in her losing her left leg. Soon after, the boy began complaining of back and leg pain and was diagnosed as having rheumatoid arthritis — at only eight years old! He was brought for prayer and after explaining to him about the possibility of a connection with his sister's injury, we prayed for his healing and bound the spirit of *vicarious pain*. The pain immediately left him, and the following day he entered and won a youth golf tournament. Praise the Lord! We need insight from the Lord to be effective against the wiles of the devil.

10.

Gate of Over-Protectiveness

It is absolutely necessary for parents to protect their children. This is one of their main roles in a child's life. However, this well-intentioned motive can be taken to extremes.

A doorway for demons to enter can be opened by overprotective parents. An overprotective parent is one who is often afraid of losing the love of the child, or who is continually anxious that harm may come to their child. The parent attempts to compensate for this by being involved in every aspect of the child's life. The child has neither privacy, nor the freedom to learn from their own mistakes. The parent hovers, usually with a manipulating type of parental fear, in order to obtain obedience. A child in such a situation is often insulated from normal social situations. He or she is frequently overdressed, over-groomed, and otherwise physically restrained. This type of individual grows up to be insecure, unable to relate to others, and very resentful of the overprotective parent. The child can acquire spirits of *fear, insecurity, loss of manhood* or *womanhood*, and *resentment*. This pattern seems to occur most frequently, but not limited, to a first or only child. Parents of an only child should encourage early and frequent play with other children, to teach sharing and the kind of social interaction that would normally be learned through life with siblings.

Parents must examine themselves to see if their protection is in the child's best interest, or if it is self-serving to allay their own fears. The overly protective parent may need deliverance from his or her own fears in order to be able to successfully relate to their child.

Through prayerful consideration, and Holy Spirit inspiration, a parent may find the proper protective hedge around their children without demonstrating fear and without resorting to manipulation. If a parent errs, it should always be on the side of protecting the child.

11.

GATE OF ABANDONMENT

Abandonment by one or both parents can create a doorway for demonic strongholds to take root. The fear of abandonment is one of the strongest fears, and one of the most basic spirits that can hold a person in bondage. It is, in essence, a fear of death itself.

ABANDONMENT WORSE THAN REJECTION

One of the most common spirits we have found to be present in troubled children, especially in those children who have been adopted, is the *spirit of abandonment*. This is one of the strongest root fears we've ever encountered; stronger than rejection, as it goes deeper into a child's soul. It is stronger because, while it does involve some form of rejection, it is actually a fear of *death itself.*

The *fear of abandonment* is actually a *fear of death.* If the parents don't love the child, or if the child perceives an absence of love and senses abandonment, subconscious fears can arise as to whether he or she will have enough food, clothing or shelter. To the child, the absence of love and protection is comparable to the *absence of life.* Thus in an atmosphere of abandonment, the inner spirit of the child says, "I'm going to die."

The child with the *spirit of abandonment* may have a dormant fear that will arise in later life. It may be an irrational fear, but it is very real to him or her nonetheless. A person fearing abandonment is like a swimmer who is about to drown; he will pull his rescuers under water while desperately trying to reach air himself.

Some children are more prone to experience a fear that his or her parents are not going to come home, or that the parents may leave them. Parents need to be sensitive to these fears and offer reassurance when needed.

There is a group of spirits that work against the child's well-being, composed of the spirit of *abandonment,* the spirit of the *fear of abandonment* and the spirit of *rejection.* We have come to see each of these three as separate and distinct demonic attacks. In order for a child to have the spirit of *abandonment,* he or she must have been abandoned at some point in the past. But a child who has not experienced abandonment may still acquire a *fear of being abandoned* through hearing of some aspect of it; perhaps, from a friend or from a classmate. Finally, any child can experience *rejection* from family, friends, adults, or from his or her peers.

As indicated, any of these three unholy, evil spirits may enter through:

1.   The death of one or both parents.

2.   When parents divorce, or if one of the parents abandons the family

3.   A child hearing about the parents of a friend dying or getting divorced.

4.   Reading stories or watching movies (or TV shows) about families in crisis.

5.   When there is constant conflict in the home

OBSERVABLE SYMPTOMS OF FEAR OF ABANDONMENT

Some of the observable symptoms that may give parents clues to the presence of a spirit of (or fear of) abandonment include:

> ➤ fear when the parents leave the house, even for brief shopping trips

> ➤ crying and clinging to the parents for no apparent reason

> ➤ nightmares

> ➤ nervousness, stress or hyperactivity within a child

We have seen this spirit manifest itself in adults in various ways. Most commonly, there is a suffocating presence in a home. Women have told us they knew that the things that they were doing or saying to their husbands were annoying, even abusive, and risked driving them away. But they could not stand to be ignored, and they would therefore do anything to get his attention — a manifestation of a *fear of abandonment.* For them, to be treated poorly was preferable to being ignored.

Along the same lines, some men panic if their wives are out of their sight for even a moment. In extreme cases, we have actually learned of husbands exercising such control over their wives so as to not allow wives to completely close the door when in another room, or even when using the bathroom — again, a manifestation of a *fear of abandonment.*

Similar desperate behavior may be seen in the child who has acquired a spirit of the fear of abandonment. The child will "do anything" in an attempt to get love, acceptance, and peace, as well as the assurance of life, food, clothing and shelter.

The fear of abandonment often remains dormant. As the person grows up, he or she often becomes able to deal with it and effectively suppress it. But then something occurs, a boyfriend/girlfriend relationship that doesn't work out, or rejection at school, or a rejection in the workplace, and this rejection triggers an out-of-proportion response. Why? Because it has struck a raw nerve in that person's soul, an open wound that goes back to childhood, and again stirs the fear of abandonment.

We have ministered to women with this type of fear in their lives who were having trouble trusting their mates. They never fully trust that the men they marry will remain faithful to them, or will continue to provide for them. In the recesses of their thought life is the recurring fear that their loved ones will disappear. This is especially true when there has been the death of a parent, or the death of a loved one.

There is also a root of *irrational anger* that can become intertwined with the fear of abandonment. We have come across this combination in cases where there was an early separation of a child from the parents, as shown in the following two cases.

CASE: CINDY & EARLY ABANDONMENT

Cindy, a college senior, came for deliverance about various strongholds in her life. In her life's story, it was revealed that she had an issue with outbursts of *uncontrollable anger*. These were not directed at any specific person but instead were random. She was generally a pleasant, happy person. However, she said, her mood could change in a flash. She told us that the problem with *irrational anger* had been with her all her life.

As we prayed, we cast out the spirit of *anger* first. After waiting on the Lord, we felt that there was a deeper root that needed to be explored.

Cindy had mentioned that when she was born, she had been separated from her parents during the first month of her life. During this time, she was in the care of hospital staff because of a physical condition discovered at birth. But she was not aware of any connection this may have had to her current struggles in life, especially in the area of fear and irrational anger.

In older children, we had noted that extended separations from parents had sometimes created a stronghold, as in the *fear of being abandoned* — we had seen this in young children and teenagers. But we had never encountered this from the time of infancy.

I explained that to be separated from parents at birth for an extended period of time, could have been traumatic for her soul as an infant. Think, for a moment, about the transition from the warmth and security of the womb, to the sudden awareness of unfamiliar, noisy and stressful surroundings, a sterile environment lacking in the tenderness and cuddling of new parents. The soul of an infant is awake and aware, at some level, of its surroundings.

Additionally, the soul of a newborn can be frightened by strangers coming and going, the medical professionals who may have to inflict pain on the child, e.g. with needles, as part of their urgent medical care. These men and women who save the lives of infants are heroes. But to an infant, the experience could potentially be perceived as traumatic to its soul.

She reiterated that the problem with *irrational anger* had been with her for her entire life. We suggested this fact, in connection to the separation from her parents in early infancy, could have been a root cause of her ongoing frustration and anger.

So we prayed against the spirit of trauma from infancy, the fear of abandonment that may have entered, and any irrational anger that may have resulted. A few minutes later, Cindy wiped the mascara from the tears down her cheek, and then placed both hands on the center of her chest and said, "I can't believe the pain and the sorrow that I just experienced within my chest, in my heart." She added, "It wasn't tangible exactly, but I felt all the pain, all the heaviness, all the sorrow, all the grief. I would never have believed it."

She told me, "I would never have believed that such grief could have started so early in life. But, what just happened to me was unreal. I actually experienced a heaviness, a hurt — for just a second — and then it was over. Now I know it's gone!" Having felt the presence of heaviness lift off her heart, and sensing the demonic stronghold broken, she knew the uncontrollable anger in her life had ended.

THE LINK BETWEEN ABANDONMENT AND ANGER CONFIRMED

Later that same day, the link between abandonment and anger was confirmed by an encounter orchestrated by the Lord. A young mother came in to our bookstore to receive prayer against a nagging, flu-like condition. After we prayed, she began to reminisce about how I had "eased her into the Kingdom."

She recounted, "I often came in, talked with you and asked you a spiritual question. You would think for a moment, and then give an answer from Scripture. I would take that answer and go to my car." She continued, "Through my tears I would say to myself, 'God that can't be right!' I would then head home and read my Bible and find out that it was correct. I would always return and ask you another question. And that process went on for about two years!"

Having reminded me of our past discussions, I shared with her that we had just encountered a spirit of *irrational anger* earlier that day, and that it had been rooted in the *fear of abandonment* from the earliest days of infancy. The young mother's jaw dropped, and her face registered shock. She exclaimed, "That type of anger is the same problem my son has!" She went on to say, "He was premature, so he had to stay in the hospital for almost a month. Today he has uncontrollable and irrational anger like you just described!"

She went on excitedly, "He can become terribly angry in an instant, with anyone. There is no pattern to it; and it is not directed at any particular person or thing. There is just this flash of momentary anger."

The Lord had just given me a well-timed, solid confirmation of the connection we had made earlier that day with Cindy. It was clear that the Holy Spirit wanted this point driven home, and that we were on to something. He was confirming through this young mother that a root cause of *irrational* or *unwarranted anger* can arise from early separation from the parents, and is related to fear of abandonment. No two cases are the same, but this was a revelation.

Revelations

• THE FEAR OF ABANDONMENT IS ONE OF THE STRONGEST FEARS, AND ONE OF THE MOST BASIC SPIRITS THAT CAN HOLD A PERSON, BECAUSE IT IS COMPARABLE TO A FEAR OF DEATH ITSELF.

• THE SPIRIT OF IRRATIONAL ANGER CAN, IN SOME CASES, BE LINKED TO THE EXPERIENCE OF ABADONMENT – AND THE TRAUMA ASSOCIATED WITH IT.

THE ROOT SPIRIT OF MURDER FROM ABORTION

There are a few other doorways for the *fear of abandonment* to become a stronghold in a child's life. One is abandonment resulting in a child being adopted; we cover adoption in the section following. The other, and far more prevalent door to this fear, is the involvement in abortion. In cases where a mother had received an abortion — or in the case of a father, who encouraged an abortion to take place — a future child may acquire the *fear of being abandoned.* Of greater concern, the future child may acquire the fear of *being murdered* by those close to him, primarily the parents.

The parents may have always been extremely loving towards the child. Yet, in the child's own spirit, there can be a stronghold of fear that senses a murderous spirit lurking within the home. This is something spiritual we're dealing with, and not a thing that can be rationally discerned. The child, in such cases, does not understand the inner sense of turmoil or torment, and acts out (or withdraws) in any number of ways.

When children are raised in the type of atmosphere where parents openly manifest hatred toward their children, the torment of rejection and fear is more understandable. But what about the home where there is love? Feelings of abandonment and rejection are not as easy to understand in a child who has not seen or experienced hatred in the home. The child's spirit, however, is able to sense the threat of rejection and hatred directed toward him or her from the latent demon of murder in the mother or father. Please note, this sense of hatred or murder is not coming from the heart of the parents, but rather from the demonic spirit and its stronghold that was established through a prior act of abortion. Often, neither the parents, nor the child, are aware of the spiritual forces at work in the home, related to a prior abortion.

A fear of being killed by the parents is extremely difficult for a parent to understand. How could the actions taken in an earlier pregnancy impact the life, or sense of well-being, of a future child? This is not logical, and does not seem fair to a parent struggling to bond with a child. Yet, as strange as this may seem, this is what we have encountered on many occasions. We have learned to never underestimate the wiles or methods of the enemy (EPH. 6:11). His methods are a mysterious force for evil — the polar opposite to the love and freedom (deliverance) and acceptance offered through Jesus Christ. Satan's goal is to bring children, parents and entire families into spiritual bondage.

The good news is that in Jesus, there is hope and there is healing, from all sins, including abortion. We have an entire book full of cases of women who have been set free from the spiritual bondages associated with abortion. Jesus did not come to condemn the world but to save it — and there is a path to freedom for parents from these demonic struggles through repentance *and* deliverance.

However, a latent spirit of murder can be present in the home even though the parents have repented of the abortion and really desired to have this child. Repentance is the first step toward deliverance, but it is not the complete step.

Below-the-surface, in the spiritual realm, a latent spirit of abortion or murder manifests itself in various ways. It may manifest as an inability to bond emotionally with a child, despite the best efforts of the parents. It may produce an intangible coldness by a parent toward their children. It may create hyperactivity and nervousness on the part of the child. Satan's goal in these instances is to create a detachment from the true bond of love and security between the parent and child.

In the worst of cases, the spirit of abortion manifests itself in the physical abuse of children. I'm firmly convinced that much of the physical abuse that is being noticed by hospital emergency rooms and trauma centers today, is a result of the epidemic of abortion in our country. In addition to outright abortion, it should be noted that there are other abortion-related options such as IUDs, foams and contraceptive pills that work by inducing an abortion. These are the same in effect as an actual abortion.

The power of the Holy Spirit can break through the atmosphere created by this demonic stronghold in the home. And Jesus longs to set both the child and the parents completely free from such a bondage. He cares about the life of the child and the parent.

ADOPTION

Adoption may involve a need for deliverance because of the abandonment involved in early life. We have encountered many adopted children who had fears related to family or security. However, I should qualify that those who come for ministry do so because they have experienced problems in the home. Not every home is troubled by fear. However, fear should always be seen as an enemy; it seeks to rob from our lives the peace, joy and righteousness Jesus came to bring (ROM. 14:17, 15:13, GAL. 5:22).

In cases where the fear of abandonment is operating, parents of adopted children often don't understand why the love they offer is not sufficient. To help them, I explain that the rationale within that child's own spirit is

> ..."if my natural parents didn't love me enough to keep me, how can I trust these foster parents, or adoptive parents, or "stand-in parents," not to leave me, or hurt me emotionally in the same way?"

The child's spirit is continually on guard against being so deeply hurt again. This can, in some cases, build an unwillingness to trust or an unwillingness to love, and thus functions as a barrier to the love between the adopted parents and the child. It may even manifest as an antagonism toward the parents, as if the child is testing to see if the parents will continue to love him or her even if they behave badly.

In some cases, we have dealt with panic in adopted children, when a parent leaves for even a few moments, something as simple as a trip to the store. It can precipitate a tantrum, or clinging to the parent, an unwillingness to let that parent out of sight. We have observed this behavior to be so strong as to actually cause the child to vomit every time the parents would have to go out for an evening. In such cases, there can be an underlying fear (a tormenting spirit) in the child that tries to reinforce the lie that the parents will not return.

Our hearts' desire is for the adopting parent to establish such a close bond of love with their child that prior wounds to the soul are ministered to. We pray that the parent-child relationship becomes so strong that it equates to naturally-born parent-child relationships. If deliverance plays a part in that process, then allow the Lord His ministry — a ministry Jesus referred to in His own words as "the children's bread" (MATT. 15:26).

Similar problems exist in a child who has lost a parent or parents to death. In these cases, the same manifestations can be observed, including clinging to the remaining parent, the adoptive parent, or the guardian. Fear paralyzes the child as he or she fights to not experience that kind of pain and terror again.

When the death of a parent occurs, our hearts' desire is for the remaining parent to establish such a close bond of love with their child that prior wounds to the soul are ministered to, and confidence and strength may return to their life. Again, if deliverance plays a part in that process, then allow the Lord His ministry — a ministry He lovingly deemed "the children's bread."

The adopted child may also need deliverance from the "double lineage" problem (as described by Sally in GATE 13). The ancestral lines of four parents (two natural and two adoptive) come into play, presenting the possibility of four potential sources for inherited spirits.

ADOPTION REQUIRES SPECIAL CARE

Some parents have related accounts of their adopted child hiding food, or taking food to bed with them or even hiding food under their bed. This is a manifestation of the fear that the food won't always be there, and that supply may be jeopardized. In addition, this could be a manifestation of the *fear of starvation*, a variation of the fear of death, also tied to the root of the fear of abandonment.

Other parents report that adopted children have stolen money or small valuables, a manifestation of that need for security. This may also be an outworking of a spirit of the *fear of poverty*. The fear of poverty can manifest in individuals who have experienced abandonment as a child, or have been adopted from environments of deprivation. The presence of these three spirits (abandonment, poverty and starvation) in an adopted child is understandable when we consider that the natural mother was, quite possibly, in a very difficult situation. For instance, she may have been:

1. Abandoned herself by the child's father, or by her family because of their embarrassment over her pregnancy (creating an environment of the fear of poverty or rejection)

2. In a financial bind and not able to see a way to keep the child (fearing or experiencing poverty)

3. Not sure where her next meal was coming from or how she was going to feed her child (fearing or experiencing hunger)

Thus the child may have inherited these spirits from the mother, or developed a propensity towards them through her emotional stresses. Even an infant can be affected, through the pressure exerted on his or her soul. Some children may have even had these experiences reinforced through the process of adoption, not knowing whether a family was going to show them lasting commitment, security and love.

While there may be challenges in the case of adoption, parents willing to extend such love and family bonding with an orphaned child are truly representing Jesus Himself to that child. Those parents are heroes in the eyes of God.

PARENTS WHO ADOPT MAY ALSO NEED
COMFORT THROUGH DELIVERANCE

Parents who have adopted children have come to see us for ministry and prayer. They were also in search of healing and deliverance. Adopting parents can experience hurts that other parents do not. For instance, if the adopted child resists their love early on, parents may wonder if they are lacking as a parent. The enemy is a liar — he is the "father of lies" (JOHN 8:44, NASB). He seeks to have these parents question their self-worth, as well as their ability to function as loving parents.

Parents of adoptive children can also experience rejection or hurt when the child expresses a curiosity about his natural parents. These hurts can compound when the child tries to find or contact his biological parents.

Then there are potentially disheartening words spoken by the child, as there so often are *with any child*. The child may, when acting out, say such things as "I don't love you," or "I hate you," as children may say to natural parents. But to adoptive parents, who are already feeling somewhat insecure in their parental role, greater weight can be placed on these statements even though they are not the true feelings of the child.

The adoptive parent, having selflessly given love, provision, shelter and nurture is doubly hurt if the child rebuffs that love. Unfortunately, the small child doesn't understand the situation, and children tend to fall in line with a self-preservation mindset when threatened with fear, especially a fear akin to death itself. Neither does an older adopted child fully grasp the great love and desires of motherhood and fatherhood, and may unintentionally or unwittingly respond as unkind towards the parents.

Upon reaching the teen years, many young people go through a rebellious stage (see PART FOUR - DELIVERANCE FOR TEENS). This is especially traumatic for the adoptive mother and father, and carries extra weight in terms of personal rejection of them and their love. Adoptive parents need positive reinforcement, so that the hurt is not intensified. We welcomed a number of teenagers into our home when our children were little, so we can relate to the trials and challenges of the adopting parents.

Do not despair, there is hope! Parents may need deliverance themselves, the freeing touch of the Master's Hand. The key areas would of ministry would be:

> Insecurity about not being the natural parent of the child

> Rejection if the adopted child is not able to adequately express love

> Frustration or exhaustion from a child's inability to bond with them in spite of all their best efforts and sincere offers of love extended.

This is certainly not the case with all parents who adopt. But in the cases where parents came to us for ministry, the parents had shown love and security to the child, and yet their best efforts were rebuffed, or rejected. This was a source of an inner wound to the adult soul.

Some adoptive parents have cried their hearts out in my prayer room as a result of having their love and efforts to establish a relationship with the adopted child snubbed or rebuffed. Often times, deliverance can come merely by seeing the truth. Jesus said, "the truth shall make you free" (JOHN 8:32). For many, a release of a spiritual stronghold occurs from realizing that it is not their love that's being rejected, but it is the hurt from within the child that is being manifested. It does not reflect on the parents' efforts to establish a relationship with the child.

Hurts experienced by an adoptive mother when her love and good intentions are rebuffed are very real. Although adoptive fathers experience hurts too, the mother is usually more vulnerable, because she is usually the one who spends more time with the child, as provider and as communicator. She is more exposed because her love is offered more frequently. Once a wound of unreturned love has been made, then future slights, even unintentional, by the child tend to be magnified in her perception.

ABANDONMENT CAN CAUSE DESPERATION

A baby girl and her mother were abandoned by a wayward and renegade father. The little girl was named Candy. As she grew up, it became visible to the extended family that the girl was desperate for the attention of a father. She was crying out for a father-figure, and she needed strong fatherly discipline.

The little girl became almost crazed if she could not get the attention of any man who happened to be in the room with her. Not knowing how to properly attract the attention of the man, she would bite another child or pick a fight, or even bite the man who was present. This little girl would do anything to be noticed by a man in the room with her.

When Candy was about eight years old, she would try to gain the attention of the boys in the neighborhood by pulling down her pants, or trying to pull the other children's pants down. Her bizarre behavior, unfortunately, tended only to make her more isolated and lonely. The neighborhood children were turned off by her behavior, and their parents, upon learning of it, discouraged them having any contact with her. Nudity, or exposure, is a common manifestation of a demonic presence (see the case of the Gadarene Demoniac in LUKE 8:27,35).

Candy and her mother became embittered, and turned inward to the point that they had almost no outside contacts other than their own family and their church. Deliverance and consistent parental discipline may at times be needed in situations of abandonment.

12.

GATE OF DIVORCE

Children who have gone through divorce often experience pain and anguish that they cannot understand, or put into words. For this reason they may seem silent and withdrawn, or display more overt, desperate behavior. We have ministered to many such children, and have seen the Lord work tenderly on their hearts and minds.

CASE: NINA – A CHILD OF CONFLICT

Children of troubled marriages often experience conflict in the home. One young woman, a twenty-four year old school teacher named Nina, had previously received pray for deliverance from us. She was the product of much trauma: a broken home, a father who was an alcoholic, and a mother left destitute to support a family of three small children. Her father died while she was still young, and this left her feeling deserted and grieved over the absence of a relationship with him.

She had received several weeks of deliverance that had begun in a deliverance seminar at a retreat, and then had continued when she contacted my wife and I for prayer against other problems that began to surface. One evening, as she was visiting our home and prayerfully discussing the deliverance that she had experienced, she said — quite suddenly — "I think I feel something else beginning to manifest!"

The manifesting spirit began to cause her body to contort. Back then, I had never seen anything like these kinds of manifestations. As she sat in a chair in our family room, she began to show signs of crippling. Her legs twisted, her hands became claw-like, as if in an advanced stage of paraplegia. And then her body began to bend to the right. Her right shoulder came within a few inches of touching her right hip! Had I not witnessed it firsthand, I do not think I would have believed what was taking place. Five minutes earlier, as we were casually talking, no one would have suspected the young woman had a problem of such incredible manifestation.

We commanded the *crippling spirit* to leave, and it did. Her muscles and joints returned to normal, and she returned to her normal posture. However, we sensed there was something else present, so we commanded the next spirit to manifest, name itself, and to come out. At this point, a guttural voice came out of her and shouted, "CONFLICT!" We commanded the *spirit of conflict* to come out of her, and it manifested violently. As she began to shake, Nina began to cry out, "I feel like I'm being pulled apart!"

It is difficult to describe. She appeared as if she was being pulled apart at the shoulders. It was as if someone had hold of each arm and was pulling her in opposite directions. Her shoulders looked as if they were going to be pulled out of their sockets! Then, as suddenly as it had come on, it was gone, and the battle was over. She was free.

She said, "That was awful! I felt as if I was about to break in two, like I was going to be split right down the middle. When I was a child, and my parents fought, our house was filled with conflict. I felt like I was constantly being torn between them." This was a spiritual bondage that had directly related to the conflict she had experienced in her family as a child. It was a profound experience for us all.

Changes are unsettling and stressful for any child, and children in situations of divorce can, at times, manifest rebellious behavior. Why? Sometimes it is rooted in a strong desire for attention. Sometimes, it may be an attempt to rid themselves of the internal pressure that is building.

There are common emotional adjustments for children who move into a new home, or new school system. Add to that the added emotional stress of a broken home, and there is much with which to cope. When a breakdown in family unity is occurring, it can — for some — be overwhelming.

A child's reaction to divorce can be as severe as his reaction to a parent's death. Aside from the similarities in terms of the physical absence of one parent, divorce is the *death of a family*. Satan has an unholy trinity of spirits which include murder, suicide, and death. Under these three are spirits that directly affect children. For instance, under murder there is abortion; under suicide there is self-hate and self-destruction; and under death there is the loss of a loved one and also the death of the family itself (i.e. through divorce). When ministering deliverance in these situations, the related spirits often act as clues as to the root spirit involved.

CASE: JEANNE - A STUNTED CHILD OF DIVORCE

Jeanne came to see me one morning when I was managing our bookstore and asked, "Do you have a message for me from my father?"

Somewhat taken aback by the question from this young girl whom I had never before seen, I asked, "Who is your father?"

She gave her maiden name and said, "You remember George W? You visited him in the hospital, and prayed salvation with him just shortly before he died."

I then recalled the circumstances. George had been given a copy of my book *Alive Again*, and read it. He had asked his wife to call me to arrange a visit with him in the hospital and to pray with him. When I arrived at his hospital room, we visited briefly and he told me that he had been a poor father. He felt extreme guilt over the hurts that he had caused his first family. He explained that he divorced his first wife and left a large family of small children.

His second wife, who was in the room with us, protested vehemently, "George, you're a good man. You've always been a good man; you've never intentionally hurt anyone. You've been a very good person." However, it was obvious that George was determined to make his confession (he was of Catholic background), and so his second wife of twelve years excused herself and left us alone.

George then continued, "I feel particularly bad about my one daughter, Jeanne, who is now living on the East Coast. She was the one who was hurt the most by our divorce, and I haven't seen her since that time. I really feel that I've ruined her life."

I explained that God's love is limitless, as is His forgiveness of a repentant heart. I then explained salvation through the blood of

Jesus, and he tearfully and joyously accepted.

Now a year later, standing across the counter from me at our bookstore was Jeanne, the daughter from whom George had been estranged for twelve years! The daughter whom he had tearfully explained to me with regret before his death. She came seeking a message or word that her father might have entrusted to me. I told her that I did not have a specific message for her, but rather a wish from her father concerning his children, especially her. I asked her if she could come back the next day when I was available to speak in more detail with her, so that we could discuss her father with her in our prayer room.

When she arrived the next day, I explained to her the best I could what had taken place in the hospital. I told her that her father's parting words to me were, "I wish Jeanne and my other children could have the blessed experience that I have just had of accepting Jesus as Savior." She then did.

Jeanne left our prayer room rejoicing over the salvation that she had experienced.

Still, there was a sadness regarding the death of her father and the missed opportunity of a father-daughter relationship. She had been burdened by guilt that, because of her financial situation, she and her husband were unable to come for her father's funeral, or more importantly, to see him before he died.

An important revelation in this case, and a telling observation about conflict in the home, came a few weeks later. A woman who was in our store identified herself to me as Jeanne's aunt and observed as we were talking, "How tragic it was that the divorce had an effect upon all the children." She then made a statement which had divine truth in it: "Jeanne and the other children of that family stopped growing emotionally at the time of the divorce."

Some children stop maturing emotionally, in part, when divorce occurs. This may be a result of their desire to shut out any further hurt. Sometimes, children of divorce refuse to allow themselves to be loved and can subconsciously make the decision to remain isolated. From that point forward these particular children remain *stunted in their emotional growth*. They are candidate's for the Lord's loving ministry. We pray that they find someone who can lovingly bring them out of childhood, and into emotional maturity in Jesus.

The child who is starved for the affection of one or both parents may continue to manifest child-like "little boy" or "little girl" spirits. Most frequently, this can be the result of the absence of love from the father who has left through divorce or death. We have found this to be a fairly common manifestation in adults who experienced such a loss in childhood. More detail about the "little girl spirit" is given in connection with the eating disorder Bulimia, in our book *Deliverance from Fat & Eating Disorders*.

Revelations

- A CHILD'S REACTION TO DIVORCE CAN BE AS SEVERE AS A CHILD'S REACTION TO A PARENT'S DEATH

- DEPENDING ON THE FAMILY SITUATION, SOME CHILDREN CAN BECOME STUNTED EMOTIONALLY WHEN THEIR PARENTS DECIDE TO DIVORCE

CHILDREN AFTER DIVORCE:
COMMON SPIRITS TO BE ON GUARD AGAINST

We often hear the complaint that an ex-husband's or ex-wife's undesirable traits are manifesting in a child who experienced divorce. Parents need to be on guard against lying, deception and manipulation by a child after divorce, especially as the child advances through the teen years. In some cases, these spirits have already been in operation in the family. One parent may have deceived the other parent, lied about an affair, or manipulated the spouse into granting a divorce. As such, the enemy is trying to extend his grip on the family from one generation to the next.

The child needs to be taught to forgive the father or mother for his or her weaknesses and waywardness. That frees the child to be who God made them to be. Forgiveness is a key to healing and deliverance — unforgiveness is like poison to the soul. It is also important for the child to understand the wiles and methods of the devil who attacks individual lives and families.

As an example, in the case of a wayward father, the mother can state to the child, "I wasn't able to help your father, because I didn't understand then what spiritual warfare and deliverance were all about. But I am going to help you!"

A spirit that could possibly need to be confronted in the child of a divorce is the tendency to avoid responsibilities. Procrastination, or not following through on responsibilities, may be due, paradoxically, to a *spirit of perfectionism* — the putting off of difficult tasks due to the pressure of doing them perfectly. These spirits may take a variety of forms identified by their manifestations, such as not fulfilling obligations, not paying bills, lack of commitment, an inability to complete tasks successfully, and generally, running away rather than facing problems.

Perfectionism is a sign that the child is under stress. It can be a cruel taskmaster that drives children (and adults) constantly, and torments them with the fear that failure may result in further rejection. The child of divorce may rationalize that loss of parental love was due to some imperfection on his or her part, and can thus be avoided in the future through getting everything right, all the time. Related spirits to perfectionism would include *stress*, *anxiety* and *nervousness*. Parents often are surprised that a spirit of perfectionism may be present when they look at the state of the child's room. Nevertheless, procrastination and perfectionism are intertwined one with the other.

Parents can help the child caught in this storm by commanding the spirit of *perfectionism, procrastination, irresponsibility* and *escapism* out of the child.

Some of these issues may be the result of a curse upon one of the parents. Divorce, and general life failures, can be *generational curses* — demonic spirits that move down through the lineage or bloodline. "Like father, like son" is a familiar saying. If the father was a failure, the son may also lean towards failure, without positive reinforcement and prayer against demonic activity in this area of his life. If the father was an alcoholic, the son may also lean towards becoming an alcoholic, due either to an inherited disposition or weakness, or an attempt at escapism. This subject is developed further in Part Four - Deliverance for Teens at the close of this book.

Dealing with these spirits and others that the child may need to confront can be especially difficult if the wayward parent is still on the scene and involved, however slightly, in the child's life.

MANIPULATION

In some cases, a child of divorce can lean towards manipulation. Although it may not be evident until the teen years, there are subtle clues along the way. Often, the child is aware of the ability to play one parent against the other in order to get his or her way. Overtime, this can result in a child appearing to be "spoiled" by one or both of the parents. On a deeper level, more is involved.

In many cases, the mother is the dominant care-giver after divorce and she can, albeit unintentionally, actually train her child to be manipulative through continually giving in to their demands. She reinforces the child's tendency to manipulate by allowing him or her to pressure her. The child may cajole, whine, and otherwise bend the rules, and will often use Dad as an ally or his absence as an excuse to get his or her way. This, of course, is a difficult position to be in for the care-giver. As the child grows into teens, this can morph into emotional threats, like threatening to leave home.

Outside of the home, this behavior may result in attempts of manipulation on classmates at school, and later on employers at work. The workplace, however, will be far less tolerant. School officials and employers are outside the family and do not have an understanding of the person's history, and are less likely to tolerate it. This in turn could further reinforce the feelings of rejection and inadequacy in the child. When the child becomes a teen, or when the teen becomes an adult, they need to be on guard against the opposite extremes of self-orientation and self-hate.

SELF-GRATIFICATION

A child who has been emotionally abandoned by a parent may lose restraint in various areas. We have ministered to adults who experienced abandonment in their childhood, where this was the case. A common example would be of over-indulging with food, especially desserts or sweets. It is common for us all, to some extent, to allay hurts by pursuing physical comfort, such as the feeling associated with sugar. Sweets are often an unconscious substitute for the absent love that should have been present in the home. Love, not sweats, ensure a sense of wellbeing. Compensating with food for the absent love of a parent is a self-destructive monster, because it causes the one indulging to become overweight and affects the facial complexion. This, in turn, increases the feelings of rejection and multiplies the hurt. It is advisable to take steps as soon as this problem is discerned to encourage self-discipline in the area of eating.

I recognize that most individuals in a divorce situation never intended to be a single parent. Many women and men are as much the victims of divorce as are the children of divorce. Parenting is difficult under any circumstances, and many families that have not experienced divorce produce broken children, as our prayer room confirms. So divorce in itself does not mean broken children. Many single parents are doing an excellent job and should be treated as national heroes. There are others, unfortunately, that are in extreme need of help.

Turmoil in the Home Can Lead to Turmoil Outside the Home

Turmoil in the home can lead to turmoil outside the home. In one case, a young boy was enrolled by his recently divorced mother in a new school. The child began clinging to the principal whenever he was nearby. He actually tore the buttons off the principal's coat as they pulled him away, in an attempt to force him to leave the school office and go to class. The staff didn't realize that the child was attempting to cling to a father figure, and were unaware of the trauma the child was experiencing at home.

Such cases can be traumatic for the care-giving parent as well. He or she may already be driven to distraction due to the nastiness of the separation and resulting divorce. The single parent now has to face new challenges such as fear of the future, fear of poverty or financial disaster, and fear of not being able to provide for the children. The stress of the situation is compounded by feelings of rejection, bitterness or hatred toward the spouse because of the divorce. While trying to cope with their own feelings of rejection, often the parent is not able to grasp or understand the emotional trauma of the children as well. The parent may be fighting their own *spirit of abandonment* after having been abandoned by their spouse. In some cases, the parent may even be a child of divorce themselves. As indicated, abandonment is a far deeper form of rejection.

13.
GATE OF BEING UNWANTED

If the mother or father rejects a child, even if only in their mind, thoughts can translate into emotions and the child may be affected on a deep, spiritual level — in the "inner man" or "inner woman" (EPH. 3:16).

No one has to tell unwanted children that they are unwanted; they know it. I suspect that their little spirits also sense it. Such children may be those conceived before the parents were married, or born before the parents felt they could afford them, or those causing career conflicts, or those necessitating moving out of a no-child apartment complex. There are an endless variety of reasons; a birth that came at an inconvenient time, or when the marriage was shaky, or after parents had decided to divorce. These turbulent times can be doors for evil spirits to harass young children. We have seen births that come late in life, or those that came when the mother was seriously ill, have an effect on the parents' attitude toward a child.

In extreme cases, the gate of being unwanted can be opened in children born to addicts, to unwed mothers, to alcoholic parents, to drug addicted parents; and yet even more, babies born to woman selling themselves to support their habits, who may not know who the biological father even is.

In certain cases, children may represent to the mother a bondage to a marriage she would have preferred to end. In other cases, women have testified that the child came at a time that prevented her from being able to join her husband while he was in the service, or prevented a honeymoon when he returned. We have encountered cases where the mother died in childbirth, and the father blamed the child, even if subconsciously, for the death of the mother. In even more painful cases, mothers have blamed the birth of the child for the husband's infidelity, or for his divorcing her. There is no end to the ways in which Satan can twist the truth and pervert it, to serve his purposes.

14.
GATE OF CURSES

We know that God has a plan for every life that He brings into existence. Satan also has designs on that life, and uses his own methods to carry out his plan. Curses are malevolent forces that are passed down through generations. Behind every curse is a demon carrying out the curse.

Prayerfully renounce and break any of the enemy's plans for the baby's life that you discern. This includes any negative words spoken over the unborn or newly born child.

"Death and life are in the power of the tongue." PRO. 18:21

BREAK SATAN'S PLANS FOR THE CHILD

The occult world would have us believe that plans are written in advance through the lines of the child's own hand, otherwise known as palmistry, or through the alignment of the stars, known as astrology, or horoscope. Through Jesus, we know better. When a parent senses a curse may be operating in a family line, it is wise to pray against a curse and destroy Satan's plan for the child. If words were spoken by any astrologist, fortune-teller, palmist, or spiritist — even words that are positive and good — these should be canceled in the authority of Jesus Christ.

A curse is a demonic force brought to bear upon a person or family by the words, will or actions of another individual. Curses are real. More importantly, they can be broken!

CASE: SALLY'S CURSES BROKEN

Sally's story was told earlier in GATE 4 - CHILDHOOD TRAUMA. Ten years after her story unfolded, we met again when she heard me speak at her church. A few days later, she called to ask for an appointment.

She said, "I know the Lord is in the process of doing something in me. He has been dealing with me and I was thinking of calling you even before I heard you speak. But the things I heard you say on deliverance confirmed what He has been showing me. I have a need to be free in a few areas of my life."

When we talked, Sally described a number of unusual problems. One problem she mentioned was a persistent problem with lack, or poverty. Sally said, "I've always had enough funds to get along, but never anything to spare. Even when I was in school as a kid, I'd have money for lunch and car fare, and maybe a dime left over. I've been working now for years, I'm in my late 30s. I've worked and tried to save money, but I've never been able to save more than a maximum of five hundred dollars. As soon as I get a little bit of money accumulated, my car breaks down or something happens to eat up whatever I've saved."

I suggested to her that this could be related to a *spirit of poverty,* and if so, was something she had most likely inherited from her biological mother, who had given her up for adoption.

In the course of describing her "just enough" problem, we had an additional thought. Through a double lineage, having both a set of biological parents and a set of adoptive parents, she wondered if she had picked up problems (or spirits) from each set of parents.

She mentioned her *fear of starvation,* which we had dealt with previously, and she observed that her weight had became a problem for her at age six when she learned that she was adopted. Perhaps, with that knowledge, her little soul was attacked by fear and insecurity, and specifically a fear of abandonment.

This spirit of the *fear of abandonment* had been reinforced on a number of occasions. One blatant and bizarre instance occurred when her adoptive mother was having trouble disciplining her and her adopted sister. The mother drove both girls back to the orphanage from which they had been adopted and told them, "Get out of the car, and go up to the door. I am sending you back."

It is positively astounding to me how brutally unkind and careless some parents can be.

Sally continued, "We both repented in tears, promised to be good, and were taken home."

Sally related another clue, "I had a recurrent nightmare as a child, until about the time I turned twelve. In the nightmare I saw body parts in a doctor's desk. In my dream I recognized the desk as being that of my family physician, and he would reach down and get something out of one of the drawers, and I could see that there were body parts in the drawers of his desk."

I asked, "Were these adult or child baby parts?" Sally replied, "Child body parts."

That gave us an indication that perhaps there was a *fear of abortion*, actually a fear of being aborted. The probability was strong that her birth-mother, who had been in a poverty situation prior to Sally's birth and who had given her up for adoption, had contemplated abortion or perhaps even attempted to get one. That gave us another area of prayer for Sally.

Sally mentioned a further point in connection with her fear of starvation. She had unnatural weight gain. She had dieted, or "starved" herself as she described, in an attempt to take off weight and had never been able to get a breakthrough. In spite of all her attempts, all her diets and all the various diet clubs and organizations she had joined, the weight remained.

I said, "Sally, let's pray now and see where the Holy Spirit leads."

We then began to pray for Sally. As we dealt with each of the things she had mentioned, she would have visible manifestations as we commanded the specific spirits to leave. She did not have extreme manifestations, but there was pressure followed by an appearance of peace as each spirit left. At the end of the ministry, she shared with me, "I felt the things leaving. As they left I saw clouds swirling around, white clouds that left. They just blew away, like someone blowing on a little puff of smoke. They were white, and I could tell that I was being delivered because they just disappeared. When you cast out the spirit of the *fear of abortion*, the clouds became yellow, then red, and then those clouds entirely left."

DISCERNING CURSES

How do I know if there is a curse on my child or my family?

Curses are usually seen in patterns of behavior or circumstances affecting an individual, a family or a group of associated individuals. In Sally's case it was a *financial curse*, a variation of a curse of poverty, that caused her to always have "only just enough" and never any to spare. The patterns of curses may also include addictions, harm to personal relationships (especially in regard to the family, such as divorce and child abuse), and obstacles to physical health. Curses can even hamper longevity of life.

I have discovered curses to be in effect when I've encountered complaints such as:

➤ Everyone in my family has died at age 42.

➤ All six of my sisters have had divorces, abortions and miscarriages.

➤ My mother was unfaithful, and as much as I hate it, I find that I have been involved with a married man.

➤ All of my brothers and sisters have had to get married due to pregnancy.

➤ Every man in my family has been an alcoholic, and now my teenage son is drinking heavily.

➤ I can not ever seem to make any progress in my spiritual life.

➤ I've either been fired from every job I've held, or every company I have worked for has gone bankrupt.

➤ My father said I'd never amount to anything, and never be successful. So far, he was right.

➤ I can't even enjoy life when everything is going well. I always seem to feel as if disaster is just around the corner and it usually is.

The individuals who made these statements all somehow sensed that these problems did not begin with them but had come through family lineage. For us to even begin to understand curses requires a restructuring of our thinking, for we are dealing with powerful unseen forces that, by our senses, we cannot understand. To reveal curses, we must turn to the only valid spiritual handbook available to Christians, the Word of God. I believe that every curse can be traced back to a broken covenant, or a breaching of its terms.

The Bible makes it clear that God takes the matter of covenants very seriously. This is in part due to the vital part they play in blessings and curses. Our relationship with God is based upon a covenant, and all covenants contain terms that include both blessings and curses. A covenant includes a series of promises or blessings that will come as a result of faithfulness to the covenant, and as an alternative, all the curses that will come upon the one who is unfaithful to the terms of the covenant.

Anyone who suspects that they may be under a curse should study DEUTERONOMY 28, where God gives a listing of the curses that can come for refusing to hear and heed His commandments. In this Scripture, we are given the "righteous curses" that are provided for disobedience by mankind to God's covenants with man. But keep in mind that "the curse causeless shall not come" (PROV. 26:2). This tells us that, while curses from one's past need to be recognized and broken, there is no need to fear future curses coming upon a committed man or woman of God.

There are, in addition, "unrighteous curses" that can come upon an individual. These would include **two main categories**:

First, there is an unrighteous curse that is invoked by an *agent of Satan*, such as a witch, a warlock, a fortune-teller or others consciously operating under the anointing or power of Satan. Practitioners of voodoo or satanic priests are examples. Frequently the one who pronounces the witchcraft curse is paid to do so, as Balaam was in NUMBERS 22, but this is not always the case.

Second, there is an unrighteous curse spoken by an *individual*, by someone who hates you, but who is unaware that the words they speak carry power from Satan.

Obedient Christians need not fear being cursed. Curses come upon those not in Christ, or upon vulnerable children whose parents are not walking with Jesus.

We have seen that other types of curses fall under these two overarching categories:

1. Curses spoken by people in the world (non-believers), *without malicious intent*, especially if you do not resist it. An example would include a doctor who says, "You'll be dead within two years if you don't quit smoking, etc." Or, a CPA who says, "Your business will fail, if you continue to tithe."

2. Curses spoken by *Christians unintentionally*. For instance, "You look like you're not feeling well… you had better be careful, you might be sick for weeks."

3. Curses spoken by *Christians intentionally*, and with manipulative motives. These amount to **witchcraft in the church**. An example would include a pastor who says, "If you leave this church, your marriage will fail and your children will leave you." We knew a person who left a local full gospel church because he discerned the bondage of legalism, and was told by his pastor: "If you leave this church, your business will fail and your prayers will not be answered."

A malevolent pronouncement can become a curse if believed, accepted or acted upon by the person against whom it was directed. The most dangerous of curses may be those which come from one's own family. We simply do not think to fight or resist them:

- "You will never amount to anything."
- "You're dumb. You will never grasp math."
- "You're overweight like Uncle Harry, you'll die young like he did."
- "You have the same type skin as your father. You'll be prone to sunburn."
- "You have the same type of hair as your grandfather. You'll be bald."
- "You have your grandmother's spirit; you'll have her allergies."

Our guard is not up around family members because we do not expect spiritual attacks from this quarter, and we tend to believe and accept as truth what is said to or about us by those we love, or by those in authority over us.

Little children who were called "bad" may find these words to become self-fulfilling prophecies in teen or adult years. "You're dumb, you're rude, you're forgetful." There is tremendous power in our words, to bring life or to bring death, to introduce blessing or to impose a curse. Our natural reaction, especially as children, is to accept or believe what we hear said about us, especially by our loved ones.

As a child, I was told so often I was stubborn that I thought it was a virtue. I thought everyone would want to be stubborn. The child's reaction may be like mine of taking pride in being stubborn. There is no incentive to fight stubbornness as long as one is proud of it or considers it to be a desirable trait.

If you have a physical impairment and a child says to you, "Uncle Bill, you sure walk funny," it may hurt because of the truth that the statement contains but it does not carry the sting of an intent to ridicule or the bite of vindictiveness. If a stranger, an adult were to say the same thing, "Gee, you sure walk funny," it would hurt far more because of the sting of the intent to ridicule, to mock or to hurt. The child's statement hurt but it was a statement made from innocence. The other example is more serious to the soul because the words were intended as a weapon, to inflict pain, embarrassment or hurt.

Unrighteous prayers are similar to Christian or charismatic witchcraft, but can also be done unwittingly. We need to pray carefully, making sure our prayers are consistent with the will of God and are not just our fleshly whims. The thought or **intention of the heart** are the keys to the words that are spoken. The prayer of "You get 'em, God" reflects our own desire for vengeance clothed in Christian trappings. "Vengeance is mine," says the Lord (Rom 12:19). Our battle is not against flesh and blood.

If we are not praying in accordance with God's will, and yet the prayer is answered, whose power is utilized? Demons are willing agents who bring to pass unrighteous prayers, and they are capable of answering unrighteous prayers by turning them into curses.

Curses come from unexpected sources. Curses are sometimes spoken over the children in the delivery room unintentionally by the doctor, who may say things like, "Boy, this kid is going to be fat." "This one is going to be ugly." Such a statement was made by a Hindu doctor who came into the labor room when my wife was about to deliver our first child. As he put a stethoscope to her stomach he said, "The baby is dead." Unaware that the child's spirit can hear what's being spoken, people often create unintentional bondages with their tongues. A good example of this is to be seen in Sally's story in GATE 4.

Revelations

- A CHILD CAN BE THE VICTIM OF A CURSE SPOKEN AGAINST THE PARENT

- CURSES CAN BE PASSED ALONG BLOODLINES FROM PRIOR GENERATIONS

- CURSES MAY INCLUDE FINANCIAL PROBLEMS, SOCIAL PROBLEMS, HARM TO PERSONAL RELATIONSHIPS, OBSTACLES TO PHYSICAL HEALTH AND HAMPERING OF LONGEVITY OF LIFE.

THE SOLUTION HAS BEEN PROVIDED

God always provides a solution for the problems that we encounter. He has done so in the area of curses, even the curses from our ancestors. One note of caution is needed when discussing generational curses: I have encountered certain groups with an *unhealthy curiosity* into unknown sins committed by an ancestor. They have an almost séance-like searching for ancestral sins.

One woman who had attended such a meeting told me in all seriousness, "Praise God, I've just learned that my great-great-great-grandfather stole a horse in the old country. The ministry team prayed and broke the curse and now I am completely free!"

The fact of the matter was she was not free. I knew she was still a gossip, lived an undisciplined in lifestyle, was a chronic complainer, her children were out of order spiritually and more. It would have been time better spent for the group to confront her known problem areas, rather than going on a spiritual trip into the unknown that was probably invalid anyway. I do recognize that on certain occasions a revelation may be granted by the Holy Spirit during ministry, several are mentioned in *Power for Deliverance*, which exposes a sin that allowed a curse to enter.

The effect of certain curses may be seen immediately, while others may take years or even centuries in their outworking. Jesus cursed the fig tree and within twenty-four hours it was dead (MARK 11:12–14, 20–21). Moses had the Israelites pronounce blessings from Mt. Gerizim and curses from Mt. Ebal. The latter, associated with curses, is pointed out to tourists today as being barren and lifeless, nearly three thousand years later!

Once a curse is invoked, it tends to remain in effect until someone greater (Jesus) comes with the power and the authority to revoke or break them. This He accomplished at the cross where He took our curses and infirmities, and defeated them. We need to appropriate the work of the cross in our lives and the lives of our children.

15.
GATE OF EXPOSURE TO CULTS, OR THE OCCULT

Not infrequently one hears of an individual who has unique supernatural powers and attributes them to God. Rather than demonstrating the gifts of the Holy Spirit mentioned in 1 COR. 12, they are instead operating in the counterfeits of the Holy Spirit — often referred to as *familiar spirits* in the Bible. There is a lack of **discernment**[2] and lack of awareness of the occult within Christian groups today, such that churches, as well as some of the most respected Christian educational institutions, have allowed these types of occult practitioners within their sphere of influence and to remain unchallenged.

Such "gifted" people may be able to levitate objects, be surrounded by a light that enables them to see in the dark, have the ability to know what is about to happen in advance or to know the future (precognition and divination), the ability to compel others (manipulation, control, domination-witchcraft), or the ability to cause things to happen in the future (spells, sorcery). Some claim to even commune with the dead (necromancy, 1 SAM. 28:7–11).

Supernatural power does not automatically mean that a person is operating through the Holy Spirit. Quite the contrary, these people are being utilized by the enemy, and exercising power through a spirit other than the Holy Spirit. There is power in both camps. But far, far greater is the power of Jesus than the counterfeits of the enemy.

Especially tragic is the individual who attends a Christian institution, is praised for the "gifts," and thus assumes he or she is particularly spiritual. This occurs even though he or she reports traumatic side effects such as nightly torments, tragedies occurring within their family or circle of friends, and ghoulish visitations. How blind can Christians be?

---

2 See *Discernment: God's Inner Voice to All Believers* by Susan Banks. Impact Christian Books, Inc. **www.impactchristianbooks.com/discernment**

It often seems that non-Christians are more perceptive of the real source of these powers than gullible Christians who have not experienced the *true gifts* of the Spirit. In some cases, Christians may fear offending someone by questioning the source of their "gift." The non-Christian is often more willing to be blunt.

All contact with the occult is forbidden to the people of God in passages such as DEUTERONOMY 18:10. Involvement in the occult, whether it is done innocently, or intentionally, is disobedience to God's Word. For one to seek help from the occult is to call upon another god (or to summon a demon). The Bible refers to it as "spiritual adultery." It insults the God who made heaven and earth, and provokes the Lord to jealousy (DEUT. 5:9).

Scripture clearly forbids man to participate in, or to seek help from, any occult sources. "Occult" actually means *hidden* or *concealed knowledge* that is beyond human understanding, a mysterious secret. Most people who flirt with the occult are not aware of one basic truth: there are only two sources of wisdom in the universe, God's wisdom and the wisdom of Satan. Thus there are only two sources of spiritual knowledge, spiritual guidance, spiritual help and spiritual healing. The power in operation behind idols and statues that can, in some instances, answer prayer is provided by a demon (1 COR. 10:20). It is demonic power at work, and always carries with it a curse *greater* than the need being answered.

Most people are unaware of how varied, diverse and widespread the influence of the occult and the demonic really are. The following partial list will give an indication, and a warning for us and for our children, of things to be avoided:

Fortune tellers, Ouija boards, horoscopes, astrology, divination in any form, water witching, tea leaves, tarot cards, séances, psychics, mediums, channelers, spirit guides, witchcraft, worship of Lucifer (Satan), white magic, black magic, clairvoyance, clairaudience, telepathy, ESP, astral projection, remote viewing, eastern religions and practices, transcendental meditation, yoga, reincarnation, spiritualism, numerology, table tipping, levitation, cabala (Kabbalah), psychic powers, pendulum healing, pendulum divination, pendants (amulets) for luck or power or healing, spells, automatic writing, palm reading, voodoo, numerology, hypnotism, superstitions or any facets of the New Age. Practicing any of these activities, or filling your mind with them by watching movies that glorify such things, can open you and your children to demonic activity resulting in a curse.

16.
CLOSING THE GATES:
PROTECT & BLESS YOUR CHILD

Parents do have a responsibility to protect their children from harm. We have mentioned the problems that can occur as a result of excesses in the area of parental protection. Both Scripture and life require a balance. We must avoid extremes.

Protection from physical harm is certainly one major role of the parent. There are, however, other types of protection required by a child. This includes protection from more subtle areas of danger that can produce emotional, spiritual or sexual harm to a child. We encourage all believing members of a family to pray blessing on the children in their care. This includes parents, grandparents, aunts, uncles, brothers and sisters.

RESPONSIBILITY TO PROTECT

We read and hear a great deal today about child abuse of both a physical and sexual nature. Parents should shield their children in so far as it is possible from pornography (in any media form) and from witnessing lewd behavior. There is great potential harm in permitting a child to see pornography, just as there is in permitting him to begin smoking at an early age, or to be exposed to the occult. Parents need to protect their child from addictions to lust, which can easily arise from pornography, and to discourage masturbation. Parents must also keep their child from situations where their child may be taken advantage of sexually by older children or adults.

Television and the Internet are constant sources of trouble for children, even when something viewed seems without offense to our adult minds. A grandson of a friend of ours became hysterical while watching a television commercial against alcoholism that showed people looking into a grave. The child's parents were in the early stages of a divorce, and his insecurities came to the surface when viewing the death scene in the commercial. We advised the grandmother to have the mother shield the child from this type of commercial, at the very least.

Children need to feel safe, and under the protection of their parents, from people and things that might cause them harm. This includes imaginary villains, like the bogeyman, or from real trouble like a neighborhood bully.

If the father is an alcoholic, the child should be protected as far as possible from his abuse — be it verbal, physical, or through the embarrassment of his actions. The child who feels that he has not been protected sufficiently while growing up will need to forgive his parents when he comes to a point of understanding. One of the most common needs for forgiveness is toward a father who has been abusive. Equally common is the need to forgive a father who was uncommunicative, with whom there has been no real relationship.

If a child is not protected from an abusive adult, whether a parent or a non-parent, he or she may become insecure and fearful, or rebellious and disrespectful.

The child will need to forgive an abusive alcoholic father, but he will also need to forgive the mother for failing to protect him from the father. This is also especially true for young girls who were sexually or incestuously molested by their fathers. Some girls have tried to tell their mothers about their misery and found that the mother was either unable to cope with the fact, or refused to believe it was occurring. We have ministered deliverance to such cases.

On a less traumatic level, the daughter whose mother was unsympathetic to her need for a dress to wear to a party such as "Prom" or for graduation, may have unwittingly caused her to be embarrassed by her appearance. The daughter will need to forgive her mother. There will be varying degrees of hurt involved. We have ministered to young women who have attained the age of motherhood who were still deeply hurt by such experiences. They had allowed feelings of shame and unworthiness, as well as feelings of anger and bitterness, to develop towards their mother, and so allowed the opportunity for corresponding demons to enter. Through ministry, the cycle of mother-daughter spite should be broken to avoid it carrying on to the next generation.

RESPONSIBILITY TO PRAY

Christian parents, as the priests of the household, have a responsibility to pray for their loved ones. Prayers can be specific! *God honors specific prayers.* One that should be in every parents arsenal is for their children to come into the fullness of salvation in Jesus and also the fullness of the Holy Spirit —its fruit and its gifts. Another prayer would be for their protection from harm.

Beautiful Scriptural promises offer encouragement and are faith-building for parents. Paul and Silas spoke a beautiful promise of salvation for the entire family of a believer when they said, "Believe on the Lord Jesus Christ, and thou shalt be saved, and thy house" (ACTS 16:31). If you feel inadequate in wording your prayers, simply use portions of Scripture that apply and insert your children's names in the appropriate places. One to keep in mind is the end of Psalm 5 —that the Lord "bless" the child and surround him or her with "favor as with a shield."

Most important of all, do not despair. There is hope! This promise from ACTS 16:31 is true, regardless of how impossible your particular situation with your child may seem, no matter how far he or she may have strayed from the Way of God. Our prayer for your child is that his or her testimony may ultimately be as Paul's...

"The Lord stood with me, and strengthened me; ... and I was delivered out of the mouth of the lion. And the Lord shall deliver me from every evil work, and will preserve me unto his heavenly kingdom, to whom be glory for ever and ever. Amen."   2 TIM. 4:17–18

RESPONSIBILITY TO BLESS

A beautiful concept from the Old Testament, which has unfortunately been lost to us today, is the "father's blessing." This is a spoken blessing from a father over his children. The blessing entails speaking of the sincerity of the father's love for his offspring and his desire for their success in the future. It requires speaking or pronouncing a blessing over them.[3] What follows is an example of what I have prayed over each of my sons.

"You are my son [daughter]. I love you and I pray that you will have a happy life, find challenging work that you enjoy, marry a good Christian girl who will be a good and faithful wife, and have children which will bless you as you have blessed me."

Children need a stable home, to know that their mother is loved by their father, and that they are loved by their parents — to the extent that this is possible. It is encouraging to know that many short term mistakes are nullified by a willingness on the part of parents to show their love, to submit themselves openly to the Lord, and to bless their children through prayer. It is also a sign of sincerity for parents to admit their mistakes, especially to the child, who is all too ready to see hypocrisy in the parent who says, "Do what I say,

---

3 See *The Father's Blessing* by Frank Hammond. Impact Christian Books, Inc.
   www.impactchristianbooks.com/frank

not what I do." Everyone makes mistakes, parents included. It is what we do about our errors that makes the difference.

"How can I create stability in my home, and how can I communicate stability to my children?" The answer is through discipline. We will address this next.

PART TWO

DISCIPLINE GUARDS AGAINST DEMONIC ACTIVITY

"TRAIN UP A CHILD IN THE WAY HE SHOULD GO: AND WHEN HE IS OLD, HE WILL NOT DEPART FROM IT."

PROVERBS 22:6

"CHILDREN, OBEY YOUR PARENTS IN THE LORD: FOR THIS IS RIGHT. HONOUR THY FATHER AND MOTHER; WHICH IS THE FIRST COMMANDMENT WITH PROMISE; THAT IT MAY BE WELL WITH THEE, AND THOU MAYEST LIVE LONG ON THE EARTH. AND, YE FATHERS, PROVOKE NOT YOUR CHILDREN TO WRATH: BUT BRING THEM UP IN THE NURTURE AND ADMONITION OF THE LORD."

EPHESIANS 6:1–4

DISCIPLINE
GUARDS AGAINST DEMONIC ACTIVITY

Jesus told His disciples before He ascended:

"Go ye therefore, and teach all nations, baptizing them in the name of the Father, and of the Son, and of the Holy Ghost."

MATT. 28:19

The word which He used for *teach* means to *disciple*. He tells His followers to go *make disciples*, that is, to bring mankind under discipline to Him and to His teachings. What better place for us parents to begin, than to bring our own children under the discipline of Christ, and to make disciples of them?

Discipline is the first step in ministering peace to a child's soul and as such should be utilized first. Discipline includes training a child. If discipline does not accomplish a longer term resolution of a problem, deliverance may be required. Discipline should be performed early and thoroughly enough to get through to the will of the child. However, children differ tremendously in their responsiveness. We had one son at whom we had merely to look disapprovingly and he'd break down in tears. The other was extremely stubborn and had a very strong will, which required discipline of a more physical nature.

Children both desire and need to be loved. They also desire to be disciplined. To children, discipline and training show that a parent cares enough to correct them and to be involved in their life.

17.
A CHILD WANTS TO BE DISCIPLINED

A child may not ever tell you this, and it may not hold all the time in all cases, but children desire to be disciplined and trained. When properly motivated, discipline is an act of love and care. Children, as they grow older, can learn to appreciate what was done for them.

Lola, who had been saved and baptized in the Spirit in our prayer room ten years earlier, came to see us seeking deliverance. She explained that her life had become miserable and she was in the process of divorcing her second husband. In the process of our conversation, after describing all her problems, she said something curious: "I realize my parents didn't discipline me when I was a child, and I felt rejected because of it." From what we could gather, a spirit of *rejection* had entered her life as a result of a lack of discipline.

"From childhood on," she continued, "I have acted in a rebellious way, in essence crying out, 'Govern me, somebody govern me! Somebody show me they love me by making me obey. I feel loveless, and I need to be loved.'"

Unfortunately Lola had sought for love in many wrong areas, and had set impossible standards for herself, in an attempt to win the approval of others. It was a terrific blow to her when she finally recognized she was not perfect and that she had limitations.

Revelations

• LACK OF DISCIPLINE CAN BE PERCEIVED BY A CHILD AS REJECTION, OR THAT THE PARENT(S) DO NOT CARE

• CHILDREN CAN BECOME REBELLIOUS IN AN ATTEMPT TO FIND OR RECEIVE DISCIPLINE AND LOVE; ACTING OUT CAN BE A FORM OF CRYING FOR ATTENTION

The Bible contains numerous passages that describe our present problems with families and discipline.

> "As for my people, *children are their oppressors...* O my people, they which lead thee cause thee to err, and destroy the way of thy paths."   ISA. 3:12 [ITALICS MINE]

> "This know also, that in the last days perilous times shall come. For men shall be lovers of their own selves, covetous, boasters, proud, blasphemers, *disobedient to parents*, unthankful, unholy, without natural affection, trucebreakers, false accusers, incontinent, fierce, despisers of those that are good, traitors, heady, highminded, lovers of pleasures more than lovers of God; Having a form of godliness, but denying the power thereof: from such turn away."
>   2 TIM. 3:1–5 [ITALICS MINE]

Tragically these two passages accurately describe the days in which we live. Our era is characterized by *disobedient children*. It is a day in which the young are indeed like the adults, meaning selfish, covetous, proud and boastful — empowered, and lacking innocence at too young of an age. We find ourselves surrounded by those who continually blaspheme the name of God, who have perverted sexual desires, who do not or cannot keep their word, who lie readily and are without self restraint, who are fiercely violent and hate the righteous. Men abound who are unfaithful, caught up with gratifying themselves and not interested in any deep relationship with God even though they may make a pretense of it to appear Godly.

These truly are perilous, dangerous times, for without any natural affection, the undisciplined and disobedient children have become disrespectful, rebellious and even murderers of fathers and mothers. Events unthinkable a few decades ago are found almost daily in the newspapers. Entire families are murdered by one of their offspring. Children callously kill classmates. Even though God accurately foretold it long ago, we ask ourselves, "How could this state of affairs have come to be?"

Some social analysts have placed the blame upon modern child-raising theories, which discourage discipline. Others have blamed the courts which have sided with the position of discouraging discipline including any form of physical punishment. These influences have reinforced the insecurity and laziness of parents and accelerated the breakdown of the family structure. Hand-held devices and their constant distractions have shortened what little time families have to bond. So has the failure of the churches to clarify issues and to denounce sin. There is now an epidemic of divorce and a rejection of the Word of God, wherein we read:

"Withhold not correction from the child..."   PRO. 23:13

My wife Sue had a revealing experience along these lines while teaching in the sixth grade in the public school system. She often noted that pupils would come to her to share almost boastfully about some disciplinary chore which the parent had required. It seemed as if the child was proud of the parent's attention manifested by the disciplinary action.

She has also contrasted the classes which she taught during her first and second year of teaching. The first year she attempted to befriend the children, being in retrospect, somewhat lax in her discipline. The next year she was much stricter. The students from the second year still come to see her, *twenty years later*. She has yet to hear from even one of the students from her first class. This spoke volumes to her about a child's attitude toward correction, as a form of care and guidance.

18.
How Do We Learn Discipline?

Recognizing that it is both essential and God-ordained that we correct our children, how do we go about it effectively? It may help to consider how we as children learned discipline:

1.) by our parents training us – before we were able to communicate

2.) by our parents instructing us – after we were able to communicate

3.) by our parents disciplining us – punishing for misbehavior, encouraging good behavior

4.) by observing our parents – as examples of moral behavior

5.) by God's grace – being caught when we broke a rule: not being allowed by circumstances to get away with it.

We may have learned some of our most memorable lessons by virtue of the example set for us by our parents, such as to be moral, not to drink to excess and to keep our word. It is unfortunate that the parental examples set for children can also be negative.

Maturity is marked by the degree of self-discipline a person maintains. Self-discipline is learned gradually in a number of ways. Although the learning continues into adulthood, the years preceding twenty-one are the *most intense*. We learn to govern ourselves by observing the example set by our parents and other role models. The rules and standards are set while the child is young in order to show him or her the way to peace, and to permit him or her to experience the benefits of a disciplined life through gradual independence. As the child grows older, the enforcement of rules is gradually diminished until he or she disciplines themselves without assistance. *Self-control* is one of the fruits of the Holy Spirit (GAL. 5, NASB).

A recent study in the field of education revealed that if a child cannot manifest self-discipline and moral values by age twelve, he or she may never do so. But through Jesus, there is hope!

19.
WILLFUL DISOBEDIENCE

We as parents are given scriptural instructions to discipline our children in PROVERBS 13:24. To amplify on a truth mentioned earlier, sin in its most obvious and flagrant form is when someone intentionally chooses to disobey God's laws — choosing to do wrong when we know to do right. The child, before he knows God personally or His rules, expresses sin in the form of rebellion in other ways. The child who willfully disobeys his parents is sinning, or rebelling, in the only way he or she knows. As the child gets older, willful disobedience may be directed toward teachers or any other authority figure, such as the principal or the police.

Parents represent God, and the parent establishes what is right or wrong in the child's frame of reference. Because such willful disobedience is rudimentary sin, and part of all our Adamic natures, it is essential that the parents confront it and counter it with discipline. Such behavior is not cute and must be disciplined.

The results of allowing the child to go undisciplined can be extremely far reaching. Eventually, in order to be saved, that child must be willing and able to surrender his will to the will of God. If his will is completely unbroken, and he has never learned to submit to the will of his parents, or to obey their wishes or direct commands, he may find himself ultimately unable to surrender his will to God.

Many "modern" parents seem to feel that to discipline children will do them irreparable harm. You may observe their children in most public places. In the grocery store you see their children handling things, opening cookie packages for instance while the parents stand by saying, "Don't do that, Georgie; don't do that. Don't do that again." But they don't enforce their words at all.

The result is two-fold. First the parents have lied to their child for they do not follow through on their threat to discipline. As a result, the child doesn't believe that he or she will be punished for misbehaving. Second, the undisciplined child becomes spoiled, by repeatedly having his or her own way.

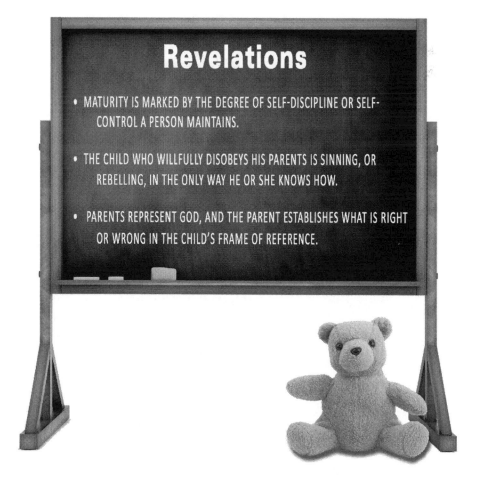

Revelations

- MATURITY IS MARKED BY THE DEGREE OF SELF-DISCIPLINE OR SELF-CONTROL A PERSON MAINTAINS.

- THE CHILD WHO WILLFULLY DISOBEYS HIS PARENTS IS SINNING, OR REBELLING, IN THE ONLY WAY HE OR SHE KNOWS HOW.

- PARENTS REPRESENT GOD, AND THE PARENT ESTABLISHES WHAT IS RIGHT OR WRONG IN THE CHILD'S FRAME OF REFERENCE.

Many parents make the mistake of placing their child's intellectual skills above all else, and treat them as equals. When this is permitted, a problem soon arises as the child begins "talking down to" or arguing with his or her parents. The same attitude shortly spreads to interactions with teachers and later employers. This attitude, if allowed to develop in the child, will also negatively affect relationships with peers. We must remember that our children become equal to us only in adulthood.

First and foremost children need love. They need to know that they are loved. Love creates a feeling in the child of wellbeing, of him or her being wanted and belonging to a family. Love is not conveyed to a child merely by giving things, but rather is best communicated to the child through deeper, more soul-affecting actions. These include holding hands, both publicly and in private, giving physical expression to your love (e.g. hugs), and demonstrating total acceptance of him or her (unconditional love).

The child also needs to be taught right from wrong. Ideally the parents should set for their child an example of integrity, courage, and morality through their own behavior and attitudes. As the child begins to confront situations in life requiring decisions, the child should be praised and encouraged for good behavior, but also firmly disciplined in love when choosing bad behavior.

Punishment can cause the child to cry. Four stages of tears may be encountered: tears of fear (anticipating the punishment), tears of anger (for being caught), tears of hurt (momentary and emotional), and finally tears of repentance.

In our family, whenever possible, I as the father did the punishing. Men normally tend to be less emotional, and better able to use restraint. The mother usually has the role of disciplinarian during most of the day while the father is at work and needs a relief.

Punishment in our family was a brief ritual which was *not prolonged*. Punishment is not sending a child to his room for an hour to pout. This tends to let resentment and anger fester in the child for that period. Although our children soon learned that punishment could hurt, it would be over quickly. Thus, it was far less brutal than the more prolonged method of punishing by ignoring the child, or by banishing them from family interaction. As a result, restoration to normal family life came quickly.

After the punishment was administered, forgiveness to the child was offered. Prayer in agreement to forgive the parent was required when appropriate, and then love and assurance of acceptance and restoration to the family unit was given to the repentant offender.

The child was not left in doubt as to whether or not he was still loved. Because the punishment was administered in love, the child learned that it was the behavior that was not acceptable, while he himself was still loved in spite of his actions. It is important to explain the punishment to the child, so that he or she knows they are accepted and loved — not because of the misdeeds, but in spite of them.

A child reared without discipline tends to feel unloved and unwanted (as in the case of Lola). Since such children feel an inner alarm, and tend to wonder at the parents' lack of concern for them, they will often begin acting in such a way as to force the parents to impose restrictions upon their behavior! If the parents do not respond, then the child's unchecked behavior will soon become more brazen or bizarre, as in Candy's case (GATE 11). A child feels a sense of protection by the restrictions placed upon him or her. To know the rules, and to know the boundaries wherein we are safe, helps us all to have a sense of well-being and to feel at peace.

20.
CONSISTENT DISCIPLINE BRINGS DELIVERANCE

Disciplining in the home should be directed by the father. When he is present he needs to do the disciplining. While he's at work or absent, the mother should carry forward the principles the couple has established. When out as a family, at a restaurant, in church, or shopping, the father should be the one to maintain order. There should be unity between the parents; *agreement* within the parental couple regarding discipline is extremely important. The child will naturally try to work one parent against the other, seeking to avoid punishment, therefore unity and agreement are essential in discipline.

It is even possible to discipline certain undesirable traits out of a child. We had one son who was accident prone. My wife became so frustrated with him returning bleeding every time he went out to play, she began to sense something more than coincidence at work. She finally threatened to discipline him the next time he had an accident. She only had to discipline him once, and he quit having accidents. This seems totally illogical to our rational minds, but there was apparently a *spirit of carelessness* that was taking advantage of him, or something along those lines.

Consistent discipline can bring deliverance! Having been consistently disciplined, a child can make a decision of his will to refrain from the wrongful behavior desired by the demon. The demon will give up on him as a target and may actually leave him alone. This is true also for lying and selfishness. By breaking an habitual form of behavior, the soul may be freed from bondage.

Consistent discipline can also stir up resentment toward the disciplining parent. When this occurs the child needs to be encouraged to forgive the parent for what may seem to be unfair discipline (too strict, unnecessary, overly restrictive) or even for fair and proper discipline.

"All discipline for the moment seems not to be joyful, but sorrowful; yet to those who have been *trained* by it, afterwards it yields the peaceful fruit of righteousness."

HEB. 12:11, NASB [ITALICS MINE]

As a part of the disciplining process it is helpful for the parent to admit to the child that he or she has experienced similar shortcomings or problems. This helps open lines of communication with the child. Admit your weaknesses to the child and ask him to forgive you for anything that led to hurt. For instance, you can ask his or her forgiveness for general shortcomings in daily life, such as "Please forgive me for being short tempered, for cursing in front of you, etc."

A parent can also help his child deal with personal relationships, or shame and embarrassment, by sharing with the child similar personal experiences: "I, too, had a problem with getting mad at my classmates at school when they teased me," or "with feeling embarrassed and stupid," or "with fantasy lust," etc.

Jesus took upon Himself our weakness as a demonstration of His humanity, and to identify with us, as His children. When we, as adults, confess (using wisdom) some of our own faults, our embarrassments, hurts, frustrations, and the associated pain, we are following Jesus' example and are exposing our own humanity. It can be very liberating for the child to learn that he or she is not alone, that this struggle against the flesh is not unusual, and that experiencing embarrassment and emotional pain is a normal part of life.

This honest sharing and opening of one's self may also help to keep the essential lines of communication open between parent and child. These frank discussions can enable the child to talk about problems openly with the parent, preventing him or her from being vulnerable to silence and shame. These personal chats bring the "armor of light" to bear upon the darkness with which Satan would attempt to shroud his demonic activities through shame.

> "Do not participate in the unfruitful deeds of darkness, but instead even expose them... But all things become visible when they are exposed by the light, for everything that becomes visible is light."
>
> EPH. 5:11–13, NASB

Flippancy, irreverence, and disrespect should not be permitted in any child. The child from the earliest point of understanding should be encouraged to respect others, and especially to respect and obey parents. There are certain things the child must never be permitted to get away with, and which require immediate discipline.

1.) Overt disobedience or rebellion against a parent; manifestations such as "talking back" to either parent; striking, kicking or biting a parent, or any such similar rebellious activity

2.) Lying

3.) Irreverence

4.) Manifesting hatred toward any of his peers, which may be expressed by putting them down, hitting or kicking, calling them unkind names, or even open hatred such as saying, "I hate Billy!"

5.) Disrespect toward non-parent adults; such as teachers, grandparents, and the like, should also not be tolerated. *A child should be protected from unfair treatment or harm by adults, but he should not treat any adult with disrespect*

The child must be taught to forgive the one who has wronged him or her. If a child has been bullied by someone else, as so often happens, he or she needs to be taught to forgive and that "vengeance is mine" says the Lord. The child needs to learn to look to God for justice. And to realize that trying to get even will only make matters worse. Through trusting the matter to God, God will handle it. God may in His wisdom convert that bully into a friend, or move him out of the school, or away from the neighborhood. We had all three happen in our children's lives.

However God decides to do it, He will do it in exactly the right way. Although it may take time, even years, God will work it out and cause "everything to work together for (your child's) good" (ROM. 8:28). However, if the bullying can't be resolved, the parent has to step in to protect the child or even remove him or her from the situation.

Just as consistent discipline can deliver and protect a child from demons, so irregular discipline can open the door for problems. Likewise, discipline that is too harsh, or administered in anger rather than love, can create hostility and open the door for demonic activity. Consistent loving discipline is needed. The child's response to irregular or harsh discipline, might eventually be:

> *rejection* — a reaction of inferiority, insecurity, shyness, or

> *rebellion* — a reaction to lash out verbally or physically towards the parents

The parent is responsible for the discipline. Since the child does not know how to resist the enemy, the parent must defend the child. Effective discipline results in a training of the will of the child to be able *to resist temptation* and *sin*. Thereby, **the child also learns how to resist the enemy!**

Discipline begins as soon as the child is old enough to understand. But training is also discipline and from the very earliest moments of life, the child can be trained. The Scripture calls discipline "training."

Consistent feeding and sleeping schedules comprise discipline for babies. The parents know better than the child how often a child should eat and sleep, therefore they can train the child to the appropriate habits. Having a regular schedule also allows the mother to spot physical or emotional problems early, because she can readily compare the abnormal to the normal. If a child frets after having a good nap, the mother knows he or she is abnormally out of sorts.

Revelations

• A CHILD MUST BE TAUGHT TO FORGIVE THE ONE WHO HAS WRONGED HIM.

• IRREGULAR DISCIPLINE CAN OPEN THE DOOR FOR PROBLEMS. CONSISTENT LOVING DISCIPLINE IS NEEDED.

• EFFECTIVE DISCIPLINE RESULTS IN A TRAINING OF THE WILL OF THE CHILD TO BE ABLE TO RESIST TEMPTATION AND SIN. THUS HE ALSO LEARNS HOW TO RESIST THE ENEMY.

Every parent is aware of the rebellious phase of development within the child's personality which occurs at about age two, and usually at the time he or she learns to say "no!" It is common for disobedience to be manifested during this age, when frequent attempts are made to do the opposite of what is requested. The child's will is beginning to develop and must be molded from that point onward.

My wife, Sue, has a subtle comment for parents of misbehaving two-year-olds who attempt to excuse their children's actions as "the terrible two's." She suggests "Just try to picture him behind the wheel of a car as a teenager, manifesting this same kind of behavior." It is crucial that the child's will be dealt with at this formative age!

21.
DISCIPLINE IS A FORM OF SPIRITUAL WARFARE AND A BATTLE OF WILLS

Discipline is a battle of the wills, and in that sense much like other forms of spiritual warfare. In fact, discipline is sometimes resisting or standing against the Adamic nature in a child, and in other cases it involves standing against the union of the will of the child and the will of the spirit(s) tempting the child to do wrong. Disciplining often leaves one feeling "wrung out," much like the similar sensation of being involved in deliverance, opposing witchcraft, trying to be a peace maker, or even witnessing about salvation to a difficult subject. The spiritual resistance experienced is sometimes exhausting.

I learned personally that discipline can be a battle of the wills when my son was two years old. He was standing at the door of our screen porch with a two inch twig in his hand, poking 1/4 inch holes in the screen. I stepped out on the porch and politely but firmly told him, "Don't do that. We don't want to make holes in the screen."

He belligerently poked it through the screen again. I slapped his hand with my right hand. Without blinking he poked the twig again, and I immediately slapped his hand again. This process continued, and I soon realized that I was engaged in a battle of the wills with my young son. And I knew that I had to win! It was a realization on my part of the necessity of his being disciplined rather than merely a contest of the wills.

To abbreviate the rather lengthy battle that ensued: he poked the stick through the screen a total of seventeen times! I, in turn, smacked his hand with mine (slapping him only with the fingers of my open right palm), but toward the end I was putting all the steam into it that I could. Finally the battle ended when he dropped the stick and walked away shaking his hand and blowing on it.

His hand had to hurt; my own was stinging. However, the significant factor was that I, as disciplinarian, emerged from the battle as victor. It was essential that I win. I could not allow this two year old to disobey a direct command and to defy authority, or he may have never respected authority. Training and disciplining isn't pleasant at the time but yields "the peaceable fruit of righteousness" (HEB. 12:11).

It is also important to instill a desire to work within a child. There can be established in a child a sense of enjoyment in work, and to think of work as a challenge or a game, not as a burden. Training children to work is the primary area of discipline in school-aged children and especially teenagers. It is an excellent way to teach self-discipline as responsibilities of work require it. Grounding teens, although a very popular technique today, is not nearly so effective as putting them to work.

Light chores can be given to young children. They need to be taught patiently and lovingly how to do their responsibility so they will be successful and take pride in what they do. Their success makes them feel important and needed in the family. This often requires more time from one or both parents but later yields self-disciplined adults. Supervision is needed, as is the administration of the promised consequences if the task is not completed. Many struggles may ensue, but consistency and keeping your promise or your word is key. "I asked you to take out the trash each day this week; I owe it to you to see that you do it" gives your child the role model of responsibility, love and faithfulness. I don't believe in loading children with chores, but each should have some tasks appropriate to his age.

Rather than grounding a teenager, I found it better to keep him at home to clean the garage or rake the yard, some task that he is not usually assigned. If he has not acted responsibly, then give him a taste of proper responsibility. Grounding is comparable to sending a small child to his room. Both give much time for resentment and boredom to grow. If the child does not do the task well, send him back to do it again, but check to see that he knows how and give assistance if he does not. Giving assistance, if done sparingly, when the child's attitude has improved can be the biggest blessing! The worker then learns cooperation, mercy and often opens up to his parent during the time of working together. Our Father in heaven required the most from us, but then gave His Most to help us (His Son), knowing we could not meet the challenge.

I once observed a cute, intelligent child of about four years of age picking up peanut-sized pieces of Styrofoam. After picking up each piece he would stop and say, "Phew, Phew!" and wipe his brow as if he were exhausted. Having picked up about eight pieces, he said, "I've got to rest."

He had himself convinced that he was tired from the little bit of effort that had been expended, perhaps the result of the influence of some negative role models. I had a momentary vision of him fifteen or twenty years later with no change in attitude, working at a laboring position and angry because he was not able to get a good job.

So I attempted to help him change his attitude by suggesting, "A big strong boy like you isn't going to get tired lifting those little pieces, is he?"

He smiled and said firmly, "No!" And then went back to "work."

The major advantage of regular schedules and chores lies in being able to detect problems within the developing child when he deviates from the expected behavior. Parents do, however, need to be flexible enough to slacken up on the chores if the child is working hard in another area, at his studies, music or a sport. The key is to be sure the child is busy with meaningful tasks. "Idleness breeds trouble" and great joy can come from finding oneself through diligent tasks.

One further point to be noted: every child has a special talent; for some it may be music, art, computers or a sport, the list of possibilities is almost endless. It is desirable for each child to be exposed to a variety of options, to be well rounded, and then develop his or her strengths. A child with a special ability has more self-confidence and a more positive self image. My wife Sue wrote a thesis at university on creativity and how to develop it in a child. Her conclusion was that creativity was there from birth. The one factor which made one creative child more successful than another was self-discipline. In other words, Mozart would have failed if he had not been disciplined to sit and work at his music!

Parents also need to realize that there is more than one kind of intelligence. Schools test in some fashion or another for the "I.Q." of a child, a test that measures the potential for academic achievement and success. However, there are no tests to measure three other kinds of intelligence: 1. creativity (which is difficult to be linked to a test score), 2. social skills (communicative abilities), and 3. spiritual sensitivity.

Look for all four kinds of intelligence in your child, and offer reinforcement. Just because a child may be slow academically does not mean that he or she cannot excel if trained and encouraged properly. Channeling a child into his areas of strength will eliminate a lot of the kinds of disciplinary problems one encounters in the case of children with "time on their hands." Avoiding idleness, including T.V., video games, or computer time, can itself prevent oppression.

Even children that are learning disabled can benefit from deliverance and healing. Hyperactivity can be due to spirits. There may be other factors as well, such as the discoveries made in recent years concerning food. For instance, studies have revealed that sugar affects hyperactivity, as do certain other food additives.

Revelations

- DISCIPLINE IS A BATTLE OF THE WILLS, AND IN THAT SENSE MUCH LIKE OTHER FORMS OF SPIRITUAL WARFARE.

- EVERY CHILD HAS SPECIAL TALENTS, AND A CHILD ALLOWED TO PURSUE THESE TALENTS HAS MORE SELF-CONFIDENCE AND A MORE POSITIVE SELF-IMAGE.

- HYPERACTIVITY AND OTHER BEHAVIORAL ISSUES CAN, IN SOME CASES, BE DUE TO SPIRITS.

CASE: POLLY AND VICTORY OVER HYPERACTIVITY

"How is Polly doing?" I recently asked her stepfather. He responded, "Polly is married now, and expecting a baby of her own."

I couldn't believe it. Upon reflection, I realized that it had been fifteen years since I first met Polly, as a seven year old. I was setting up for our regular Thursday night meeting in the basement of the public library, in a room where we used to meet. I was arranging the tape recorder and my Bible on the table that I used as a podium, when suddenly a sweet little face with long tousled hair and inquisitive eyes peeked up over the table's edge. The little girl asked sweetly, but slightly impatiently, "Mr. Banks, can I be healed now?"

This I realized must be Polly. One of the couples who had been attending these meetings called earlier in the day to ask if we would pray for their daughter at the end of the meeting. Polly, they explained, was extremely hyperactive and was in a special school district for children who were beyond the scope of a normal classroom. Polly's natural father had abandoned her and her mother when she was just an infant. Her mother had remarried a year or so later.

Her mother related to me over the phone, "Polly is now so hyperactive that she can't sit at her desk in the classroom. She keeps getting up and moving around the room. They have told us they aren't sure they can keep her, or even if she's educable. But we know with God all things are possible."

After the singing, worship, a time of waiting on the Lord, sharing, and the teaching portion of the meeting, we would break at about 9 p.m. to allow the people who didn't wish to remain for the healing service to leave. As soon as we had opened the healing portion of the meeting with prayer, we invited Polly to come forward. We prayed for healing for her from anything that would prevent her being able to learn, or to be calm at school. Then we bound and commanded the hyperactive spirit to leave her, along with every other spirit that caused her to be unable to be still and at peace. It was a pleasant time of ministry.

Polly's mother kept me informed of her subsequent progress. The very next week she reported, "Polly has been able to stay in her seat at school, and all the teachers are amazed at the change in her. She seems to be really at peace."

The next time I heard from her, she reported that Polly, after completing the semester at the special school, was returned to a normal public school, and did very well. Now her father told me that she is expecting a child of her own. God truly does provide for His children.

"Having seen the many ways that problems can enter, and having recognized problems in my children, what can I do to help set them free? How do I go about it?" We cover this next...

PART THREE

THE MECHANICS OF MINISTERING TO CHILDREN

"AND WHEN HE WAS COME INTO THE HOUSE, HIS DISCIPLES ASKED HIM PRIVATELY, WHY COULD NOT WE CAST HIM OUT? AND HE SAID UNTO THEM, THIS KIND CAN COME FORTH BY NOTHING, BUT BY PRAYER AND FASTING."

MARK 9:28–29

"AND HE WAS SAYING TO HER, 'LET THE CHILDREN BE SATISFIED FIRST, FOR IT IS NOT GOOD TO TAKE THE CHILDREN'S BREAD AND THROW IT TO THE DOGS'... AND HE SAID TO HER, 'BECAUSE OF THIS ANSWER GO; THE DEMON HAS GONE OUT OF YOUR DAUGHTER.'"

MARK 7:27, 29, NASB

"THESE SIGNS WILL ACCOMPANY THOSE WHO HAVE BELIEVED: IN MY NAME THEY WILL CAST OUT DEMONS..."

MARK 16:17A, NASB

The Mechanics of Ministering to Children

22.

Jesus Teaches How to Deliver a Child

After He had come down from the Mount of Transfiguration, Jesus rebuked his disciples for being unable to minister deliverance to a young boy. Following their failure recorded in the ninth chapter of Mark, He personally presents, for the edification of those around Him (and for ours), a demonstration of deliverance for a child:

> "And one of the multitude answered and said, Master, I have brought unto thee my son, which hath a dumb spirit; and wheresoever he taketh him, he teareth him: and he foameth, and gnasheth with his teeth, and pineth away: and I spake to thy disciples that they should cast him out; and they could not.
>
> He answereth him, and saith, O faithless generation, how long shall I be with you? how long shall I suffer you? bring him unto me. And they brought him unto him: and when he saw him, straightway the spirit tare him; and he fell on the ground, and wallowed foaming. And he asked his father, How long is it ago since this came unto him?
>
> And he said, Of a child. And ofttimes it hath cast him into the fire, and into the waters, to destroy him: but if thou canst do any thing, have compassion on us, and help us. Jesus said unto him, If thou canst believe, all things are possible to him that believeth. And straightway the father of the child cried out, and said with tears, Lord, I believe; help thou mine unbelief.
>
> When Jesus saw that the people came running together, he rebuked the foul spirit, saying unto him, Thou dumb and deaf spirit, I charge thee, come out of him, and enter no more into him. And the spirit cried, and rent him sore, and came out of him: and he was as one dead; insomuch that many said, He is dead.

But Jesus took him by the hand, and lifted him up; and he arose.

And when he was come into the house, his disciples asked him privately, Why could not we cast him out? And he said unto them, This kind can come forth by nothing, but by prayer and fasting."

MARK 9:17–29

It is faith-building for me, and assures me of my authority in Jesus' name, when I use a scriptural procedure or methodology. As we analyze this example from the ministry of Jesus, we observe indications of the methods that were employed by Jesus. Since He is our pattern, we seek to learn from Him and to follow His example. In this particular occasion of ministry to a child, we notice a number of steps.

1. He received a presentation of the child's need described by a parent (verse 17).

2. Jesus relied upon the description of the child's behavior by a parent or guardian, when perhaps the subject could not speak for himself (verse 17–18).

3. Jesus also used physical observation of the child (verse 20). When closely observed, demons get stirred up and sometimes manifest themselves.

4. Jesus also employed a method of inquiry, asking questions to determine when the demon first manifested, and to determine when it had entered the boy (verse 21). The Greek definitions according to Strong's Exhaustive Concordance help clarify two parts of this passage, the phrase "of a child" means from infancy, and the word for "child" means half-grown child. Since the Jews considered manhood to occur at age thirteen, half that age means the boy was probably seven years old.

5. Jesus offers an encouragement for faith to believe, which assures that the deliverance was both possible, and at hand (verse 23).

6. He rebuked the spirit by name, in this case "dumb" or speechless. This was obvious even to the parent because it caused the child to be unable to speak (verse 25).

7. Jesus also received a Holy Spirit revelation, because He also rebuked a deaf spirit (verse 25).

8. Jesus spoke the command "to come out and to never enter again" (verse 25).

9. The spirit's reaction was violent. After it had torn the boy, another spirit attempted to camouflage its existence as a spirit of death (verse 26).

As a commentary on this experience, I too have witnessed the *spirit of death*, where people being delivered collapse as if dead, just as the boy did in this Bible verse. The first time I encountered this spirit, I was hit with the fear that a woman was actually dead. But having on the armor of righteousness, knowing that we had done nothing wrong, and that we were ministering in Jesus' name, the fear was more easily resisted. We quickly rebuked the *spirit of death*, and cast it out. As soon as we did, the color returned to her face, and we helped her to her feet.

10. In addition, Jesus ministered a *healing* touch to lift the boy (verse 27), and then the boy was able to arise himself. Our idea that healing was administered is confirmed by the parallel verse in Luke 9:42b which tells us: "And Jesus rebuked the unclean spirit and *healed* the child, and delivered him again to his father."

11. Jesus responded to the disciples' question regarding their impotency by explaining that "this kind" of demon is different — it was a strongly entrenched, long established spirit, which had physically manifested in a powerful way in the boy's life. Jesus told them that this kind can be cast out only by *prayer* and *fasting*. Thus, He indicates that the one ministering needs to prepare himself for spiritual battles in advance, by means of prayer and fasting, (verse 29).

Because the boy's deliverance need was immediate, and obviously did not allow for such prolonged preparation on the spot, Jesus is clearly telling His hearers that those who engage in deliverance ministry need to be in a *constant state of preparedness*. That means to be praying and fasting regularly, in order to be prepared before a need arises. I find the disciples didn't fast while the Lord was with them in the flesh:

> "Then came to him the disciples of John, saying, Why do we and the Pharisees fast oft, but thy disciples fast not? And Jesus said unto them, Can the children of the bridechamber mourn, as long as the bridegroom is with them? But the days will come, when the bridegroom shall be taken from them, and then shall they fast."
>
> MATT. 9:14–15

In this hour, perhaps as never before in the history of the world, there is a need for the delivering power of God to be manifested — that the prison doors be battered down with spiritual weapons, and that those who are in chains, bruised and wounded, be set free.

Jesus loved the little children. He might approve of our reading a familiar quotation from Him, with an added emphasis for ministering to children:

> "The Spirit of the Lord is upon me, because he hath anointed me to preach the gospel to the poor [little children]; he hath sent me to heal the brokenhearted [children], to preach deliverance to the captives [children & teens], and recovering of sight to the blind [parents of children], to set at liberty them that are bruised [and have been abused]."
>
> LUKE 4:18 [BRACKETS MINE]

CASE: JOHNNIE'S DELIVERANCE

One evening we were invited to have dinner with friends at their home. After dinner, we were sitting in their living room chatting, when a paper airplane flew into the room and landed on the rug in front of us. Their adopted son, Johnnie, yelled down from upstairs, "Read it."

His mother opened the paper and found a note asking Sue and I to pray with him. She exclaimed, "Praise the Lord! Johnnie has never asked anyone outside our family to pray for him!"

The parents brought Johnnie to us and we asked what he wanted us to pray with him about. He said, "I want to have the things that make me have 'troubles' get out of me."

I mentally reviewed what we knew of Johnnie's case: he was 11 years old, had been adopted shortly after birth, and had problems including stuttering and difficulty relating to others, perhaps due to a fear of ridicule. He had been hampered in his schoolwork as a result of these problems. Although the family felt that his problem was emotional in origin, many others suspected that he was mentally impaired.

It was quite a deliverance session with Johnnie. We were tired and would gladly have stopped at any point if it had ceased to be productive, but spirits kept manifesting one right after another.

We let Johnnie take the lead; as soon as he had named a problem, we would then command it to leave him. Children often don't know the technical names that adults use, but that need not impede the deliverance. Johnnie had a limited vocabulary, which coupled with his speech impediment, made communication somewhat difficult at first. His list of names for the spirits tormenting him went something like this:

"The thing that makes me say bad things to my teacher,"

"The thing that makes me want to hurt my sister,"

"The thing that makes me stutter,"

"The thing that makes me cuss,"

"The thing that causes me to be mad at people at my school."

He would have visible manifestations, but most frequently he would feel a presence move through his stomach and out his thorat. He would say "I feel it moving in my stomach. . . it's coming up into my throat ... it's gone!" and "It's in my back; moving up my back into my head; it just went out the top of my head!" and "It's just gone out of my heart." As he indicated that he felt the presence leave, and the associated pressure gone, we would go on to the next spirit, commanding it to name itself. The spirits would reveal their presence to him and then he would identify them to us, by their nature or effect on him.

One of the most heart-wrenching spirits he named was "The thing that makes me drop balls, and people laugh at me." We commanded this spirit that caused his lack of coordination to leave him, again simply using his own terminology.

Finally, he said, "I don't feel anything pushing inside me any more." We reviewed the situation with his parents who had been supporting us with prayer. They said, "We can't believe that you've prayed with Johnnie for hours. No one in the world would believe this. We can't thank you enough."

We appreciated their expressions of gratitude, but the report we received the next afternoon was of far greater reward. His mother called to report, "Johnnie went out and played football this afternoon with his father; he was able to catch the ball for the first time in his life!"

Spirits can, in some instances, cause physical conditions and this fact is established in the thirteenth chapter of LUKE. This account records the crippled woman whom Jesus healed by casting out a *spirit of infirmity*. So in some instances, there may be spiritual forces at work behind physical conditions.

The promise for deliverance from physical sicknesses and diseases is given to us, as believers, in the same major commissioning in which Jesus gave His church the power to cast out spirits:

> "And these signs shall follow them that believe; In my name shall they cast out devils; they shall speak with new tongues; They shall take up serpents; and if they drink any deadly thing, it shall not hurt them; they shall lay hands on the sick, and they shall recover."   MARK 16:17–18

Revelations

- SOME SPIRITS MAY BE MORE ENTRENCHED THAN OTHERS, EVEN IN THE CASE OF A CHILD.

- THERE IS, ON OCCASSION, SUCH A THING AS A "SPIRIT OF DEATH" WHICH CAN BE CAST OUT OF A PERSON.

- SPIRITS CAN CAUSE PHYSICAL CONDITIONS, INCLUDING POOR SKILLS.

"This all seems so overwhelming. I know that my child has been hurt and is hurting now, but where and how do I begin?" We cover this next...

23.
HOW TO PRAY FOR DELIVERANCE

The first step in deliverance is to forgive. Each parent should do a self-analysis to determine who needs to be forgiven. If there has been a divorce, or abandonment experienced by the single parent, then an ideal point to begin is by forgiving the ex-partner. It will be very difficult to expect your child to forgive the absent parent if you have not, even if your bitterness is not obvious to him.

If the child was conceived out of wedlock, or marriage never took place, the sin involved should be repented, and confessed to Jesus in order that the parent might personally experience cleansing and forgiveness before commencing. Perfection on the part of the parent is not a prerequisite by any means, but obedience is.

Having cleansed your flesh from unforgiveness, dare to step out and attempt to minister to your child.

Keep in mind that Peter would never have known that the Lord's power could keep him from sinking into the waves had he not made the decision to step out of the boat. Theories are fine but as the old cook said, "The proof is in the tasting." For truth to be of any benefit to us, it must become experiential!

PARENTS ARE IDEAL MINISTERS

I believe parents are the most logical ones to minister to their child because they are the "priests of their own home." They are a church, "for where two or three are gathered together in my name, there am I in the midst of them," (MATT. 18:20). Parents have scriptural commands to pray for their children.

The simplest ministry is to the infant or very small child, because his or her will has not yet been fully developed. Therefore, the child's will is unable to fully act on its own behalf. The conflict in the deliverance is primarily with the demonic stronghold, because the mind, will and intellect of the child are not yet involved. This is extremely important, for the child's own personality, its soul, has not yet come into agreement with the evil spirit. Scripture states,

"Can two walk together, except they be agreed?" (Amos 3:3). Early deliverance, when needed, will permit a healthy development of the soul (the mind, will, and emotions) of the child, and will prevent agreement with, or acceptance of, the intruding spirit.

One of the most simple, yet effective techniques for ministering to children regardless of age, is to pray over them *while they are sleeping*. Since we "wrestle not against flesh and blood" but rather with the demons that are causing the insecurity or torment, the soul of a child can be ministered to while the child is sleeping. The spiritual forces looking on can hear us even when the child is asleep, so this offers one of the least complicated forms of deliverance ministry.

MINISTERING TO A SLEEPING CHILD

This is a sample prayer for the deliverance of a sleeping child:

"Lord Jesus, we come to You, for I know that You are the Savior and Deliverer of this child. (1) As the parent of [CHILD'S NAME], (2) we thank You for him (or her), and acknowledge their life to be a blessing from You. (3) Now, in the power of your name, (4) we bind (5) the spirit of [e.g. NIGHTMARES], (6) which has been causing torment and fear, and (7) we command it to come out of him (her). (8) We loose this child now from the hold of the spirit of [e.g. NIGHTMARES] (9) for it is written "whatsoever we loose on earth is loosed in heaven." (10) We ask You, by your Spirit, to replace [e.g. NIGHTMARES] with peaceful, pleasant sleep and sweet dreams. Thank You, Lord Jesus, for your ministry to [CHILD'S NAME].   Amen."

Let me briefly explain or analyze the elements of this prayer:

1. As parent(s) you are the priests of your home, and the ones who are legally and spiritually responsible for your child.

2. Thankfulness expressed to God for the child reminds both us and your child's sleeping (yet hearing) spirit of our love for him or her.

3. The power invoked resides in the Name and authority of Jesus.

4. We *bind* the demonic spirit in Jesus' Name, like an animal being tied up.

5. We specify, if we are able, the spirit by its name.

6. We also identify it by its nature, function or manifestation.

7. The command is given to cast it out.

8. Just as we have bound the spirit, so we can *loose* our child to be free from its grasp, in Jesus' Name and in His authority.

9. It is both advisable and faith-building to state a Scriptural basis or precedent for the action taken. If the targeted spirit happens to have been mentioned in Scripture, we might quote from the applicable passage, for instance.

10. If appropriate, it is good to pray for a healing of the area which may have been wounded by the spirit's activity. Always bless the child.

Remember, Jesus is the Deliverer. The deliverance is not dependent upon our eloquence, or our use of the right words, but rather upon the loving, compassionate ministry of the true source of all deliverance, Jesus Christ.

There is no fixed formula or rigid rules in regard to ministering to a child. I have learned what is given here by experience and searching the Scripture. Let the Holy Spirit be your guide as you minister with love and compassion. Each child is unique; each has a unique personality. Every child has had a mixture of experiences, some positive and some negative, which have contributed to the construction of his or her personality.

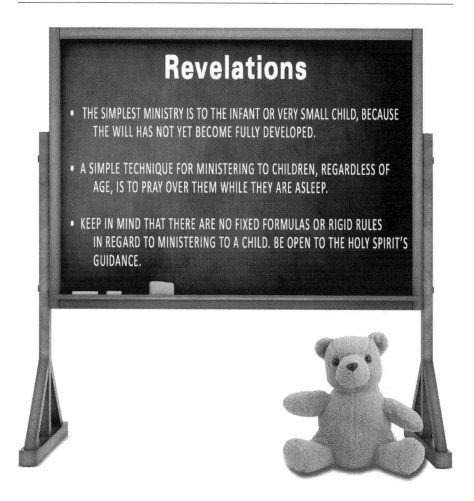

Revelations

- THE SIMPLEST MINISTRY IS TO THE INFANT OR VERY SMALL CHILD, BECAUSE THE WILL HAS NOT YET BECOME FULLY DEVELOPED.

- A SIMPLE TECHNIQUE FOR MINISTERING TO CHILDREN, REGARDLESS OF AGE, IS TO PRAY OVER THEM WHILE THEY ARE ASLEEP.

- KEEP IN MIND THAT THERE ARE NO FIXED FORMULAS OR RIGID RULES IN REGARD TO MINISTERING TO A CHILD. BE OPEN TO THE HOLY SPIRIT'S GUIDANCE.

Parents have their own ways of relating and interacting with their children based upon their unique personalities. The child is influenced both by what he has learned from them, and by what he has seen them do in the home environment.

It's very helpful for the mother or father to explain to the child about deliverance, perhaps sharing the benefits of their own experience in terms the child can grasp. "You remember how I used to be so crabby and angry and now I'm not anymore?" This helps make deliverance acceptable to the child and builds the child's interest and desire for his or her own deliverance. We also recommend the illustrated children's book called *The Little Skunk* as a means of explaining deliverance in a non-frightening way to children.[4] We will incorporate the idea of demonic forces as "little skunks" in the rest of this section.

DELIVERANCE IS AUTHORITY EXERCISED

All deliverance is simply authority exercised. Each time a demon is cast out in the name and by the power of Jesus, it is a demonstration of the superiority of the kingdom of God over the kingdom of Satan. Parents seeking to minister to a child need to keep in mind the truth of the Scripture,

"For though we walk in the flesh, we do not war after the flesh: (For the weapons of our warfare are not carnal, but mighty through God to the pulling down of strong holds;) Casting down imaginations, and every high thing that exalteth itself against the knowledge of God, and bringing into captivity every thought to the obedience of Christ."   2 COR. 10:3–5

Thus, for one to be successful in the ministry of deliverance, one must recognize:

• The authority that exists in the Name of Jesus,

• The superiority of the power vested in that authority over the power of the demonic realm (1 JOHN 4:4), and

• The faith to exercise that authority in an actual situation of spiritual warfare.

We are overcomers, and more than overcomers, because Jesus has given us dominion, and has told us to "occupy until [He] comes" (LUKE 19:13).

4 *The Little Skunk – a Children's Book*, by Sue Banks, Impact Christian Books, Inc.
    www.impactchristianbooks.com/skunk

"These signs will accompany those who have believed: in My name they will cast out demons, they will speak with new tongues; they will pick up serpents, and if they drink any deadly poison, it will not hurt them; they will lay hands on the sick, and they will recover."

MK. 16:17–18, NASB

Adam was given dominion to rule the earth, but it was natural dominion. Ours is a dominion superior to that of Adam's. We have a new and better covenant, and have been given a broader dominion, this time over the unseen forces that would seek to influence mankind *as well as* the natural world.

There is a basic truth of dominion; the *exousia* of an individual believer (the Greek word for authority) and the *dunamis* of the Holy Spirit (the Greek word for power) must be exercised. We are to take, or extend, the kingdom of Jesus Christ by force, utilizing the spiritual weapons provided to us by the Lord Himself. God's most powerful weapons have been entrusted to us. The blood of Jesus, the Name of Jesus, the keys of the Kingdom, and the gifts of Holy Spirit are weapons and supernatural tools that Jesus has provided. Thus, we have offensive weapons with which to attack Satan and his kingdom: the Sword of the Spirit (the spear of praying in the Spirit – EPH. 6:11), binding and loosening, and *exousia* and *dunamis*.

We also have defensive weapons, those listed in EPH. 6 including the helmet, the shield, the breastplate and our legal commissioning, "behold I give unto you power." He has given us His strength. In the Old Testament, they were told "Let the weak say I am strong." Paul said, "I can do all things through Christ who strengthens me."

Another powerful weapon is His Word. In the Old Testament, "God sent His Word and healed them." In the New Testament, Jesus the Word, came and healed all with whom He came in contact. Jesus spoke the word of power, and that word did not return to Him void. Now, He has commissioned us who believe in Him as soldiers in His army, giving us the legal right to use His Name, His power and His weapons.

What are the purposes of our warfare?

1.   To extend the kingdom, by adding souls to it (MATT. 24:14).

2.   To set at liberty the prisoners of war, the "captives" (LUKE 4:18).

3.   To break demonic strongholds by binding & loosing (MATT. 16:19).

4.   To "earnestly contend for the faith" (JUDE 3:6).

5.   To "Fight the good fight of faith" (1 TIMOTHY 6:12).

The Kingdom of God exists wherever hearts love, desire, and are in submission to the King — Jesus. A person is either in one kingdom or the other by default. To choose not to enter the Kingdom of God is to choose to remain in bondage to the Kingdom of Satan. Without salvation, one remains by default in the kingdom of Darkness (JOHN 1:4). We who believe in Jesus have, however, been translated into the kingdom of God's dear Son; that is, the Kingdom of Light.

The many instances in Scripture where Jesus ministered to children, taken with the characteristic aspects of Jesus' ministry, show His loving, compassionate, concern for little children. As do the following statements that He made in Matthew:

> "Let the children alone, and do not hinder them from coming to Me; for the kingdom of heaven belongs to such as these."
> MATT. 19:14, NASB

> "... whoever causes one of these little ones who believe in Me to stumble, it would be better for him to have a heavy millstone hung around his neck, and to be drowned in the depth of the sea."
> MATT. 18:6, NASB

> "Take heed that ye despise not one of these little ones; for I say unto you, that in heaven their angels do always behold the face of my Father which is in heaven."
> MATT. 18:10

The angels, perhaps "guardian angels," of little children continually behold the face of God. Jesus is concerned about the welfare of His little ones, and He has chosen to involve His angels and His earthly followers in His ministry to children.

EXPLAINING DELIVERANCE TO SMALL CHILDREN

The one ministering to the child should be familiar with forgiveness and be able to explain it in terms understandable to the child. A complete, yet simple explanation of forgiveness is to be found in some of our other books *Power for Deliverance: Songs Of Deliverance* and *Ministering To Abortion's Aftermath.*[5]

It is helpful to try to put oneself in the child's place, to try to think like the child. The young child doesn't need to know, nor would be interested in, the theology of deliverance. The child just wants to know what he or she needs to do to be free of fear and torment. The best rule is to keep it simple.

Children today have seen so many frightening movies and television shows about demons and the occult that if we were to use the word demon with some, they might be truly frightened. As mentioned, you may refer to the children's book *The Little Skunk*[6] as one way of explaining deliverance in a non-threatening way. We suggest parents read the book first, and then together with their child prior to proceeding with prayer.

DEALING WITH AN OLDER CHILD

When dealing with a more mature child, the situation is different. He or she is able to cooperate with you in a pre-deliverance session, or conversation, by explaining to you how the "thing inside" bothers them. The child can at least give you a clue as to its nature or identity, and may even be able to give you the exact experience that allowed

---

5 *Ministering to Abortion's Aftermath* and *The Power for Deliverance,* by Bill and Sue Banks. Impact Christian Books, Inc. **www.impactchristianbooks.com/banks**

6 *The Little Skunk* by Sue Banks, as mentioned previously. **www.impactchristianbooks.com/skunk**

the spirit to enter. For example, "Cousin Bobby locked me in a dark closet," or "Uncle Charlie touched me." A child who says, "My pet dog was killed because I didn't keep him on the leash," includes a lot of information about the demonic stronghold in his or her life: there may be spirits of pain, loss, grief and guilt, all in one brief sentence.

"I'm afraid because I broke Mama's vase," or "I borrowed Daddy's screwdriver and lost it," or "I looked at Tommy's book of dirty pictures, and now I have bad dreams and can't sleep" are all statements indicating the events (or doorways) by which the spirit gained entry.

The problems described may truly be serious, or seem totally innocuous to our adult minds, but the key lies in the perception of the problem by the child. Satan uses the child's perception of guilt and self-blame to work his wiles upon the innocent.

In the case of talking children, just as with adults, beware that the enemy will attempt to delay the inevitable deliverance by stalling, extending the conversation or dragging out the details of the problems. When talking with the child, you may reach a point in the conversation where further discussion is stirring up fears. You may have to tell the child, "Okay, we've talked enough about the problem. Now I want to deal with the solution. I'm going to command the "little skunks" that have been causing you to be afraid, to have nightmares, and to be unable to sleep at night to come out. You just be still, and ask Jesus to set you free, and let me pray for you."

You then cast out the appropriate spirits. Sometimes it is helpful, and you may feel led, to have the child get involved in the process by telling him, "Take a deep breath and blow it all out." On other occasions, you may just want him or her to sit still, and relax while you do the praying.

If the child is old enough to be actively involved, I have him or her personally command the thing, the "little skunk," to leave in Jesus' name. This accomplishes three things. First, it gets the child's will directly involved in the deliverance process. Second, it causes the child to realize that the power for deliverance is in Jesus' name. And third, it teaches the child how to begin doing spiritual warfare on their own.

Revelations

- PROBLEMS MAY BE SERIOUS, OR SEEM TOTALLY INNOCUOUS TO OUR ADULT MINDS... THE KEY LIES IN THE PERCEPTION OF THE PROBLEM BY THE CHILD.

- IF THE CHILD IS OLD ENOUGH, I HAVE HIM OR HER PERSONALLY COMMAND THE "LITTLE SKUNK" TO LEAVE IN JESUS' NAME. THIS GETS THE WILL OF THE CHILD DIRECTLY INVOLVED IN THE DELIVERANCE PROCESS, CAUSES THE CHILD TO REALIZE THAT THE POWER FOR DELIVERANCE IS IN JESUS' NAME, AND IT TEACHES THE CHILD HOW TO BEGIN DOING SPIRITUAL WARFARE ON THEIR OWN BEHALF.

24.
When to Minister Deliverance

The best time to treat a flesh wound is as soon as possible after it occurs. We apply antiseptic to a wound to avoid germs of infection entering, to prevent spreading of the infection and its destructive corruption. The same is true of wounds to the soul. It is best to treat them as soon as we realize they have occurred, to prevent the wound (the wrong done) from allowing a germ (a spirit) to enter, and to block the corruptive, destructive spread of an infection (the spirit's torment). We need to cast the spirit out, much like we would seek to sterilize the germs in a natural wound with antiseptic. We should be lovingly firm in our determination to minister to the emotional or spiritual wounds of our children, rather than simply ignoring them — and hoping they will go away. I am sure that on occasions, as a child, I cried and begged my mother not to pour iodine or peroxide into my cuts. But my mother knew it was necessary to prevent infection. In much the same way, we need to be lovingly firm in our resolve to minister to our children's spiritual needs.

It is possible for an infant (within or outside of the womb) to be protected from demons, and even delivered... while still in the womb. If, for example, the mother had seriously considered abortion, had mentally or emotionally rejected the child, she can repent of her rejection of the child and ask God's forgiveness. Then she should bind the spirits of rejection in the child, and cast them out along with any other spirits of hurt, fears of being unwanted, abandonment and the fear of being killed by the parents.

Even if the child was unwanted, or abortion had seriously been considered, it is still possible for the child to be delivered from the point of conception onward. There may be spirits of miscarriage, spirits of still-birth, and even childlessness (barrenness) within the mother that need to be confronted.[7] The former two pose an obvious threat to the well-being of the child.

---

7 See *Deliverance from Childlessness*, by Bill Banks. Impact Christian Books, Inc.
  www.impactchristianbooks.com/banks

The easiest time to minister deliverance to a child is probably from birth to about age two. Because the child's will is not developed, we need only battle the "little skunk" (i.e. demon) which does not have access to either a mature mind or mature will with which to resist. The deliverance is definitely facilitated, too, if the parents are in complete agreement and properly prepared.

25.
WHERE TO MINISTER DELIVERANCE

Most often, the ideal conditions for the deliverance of a child exist in the child's own home, with the parents doing the ministering. The next best option is for the one ministering to do it in the home. But that, of course, is not a prerequisite either. It can happen in a church, in a prayer room or even in an open meeting. It can also happen long distance, as by phone.

The parents should be encouraged to keep deliverance in perspective. They should be warned that a child will definitely not attain perfection merely by being delivered. Discipline will still be required, and never forget that your child is still a child. He or she is still apt to manifest, at times, childish behavior. As the child's will develops, the Adamic nature will still cause misbehavior. By all means, allow your child to still be a child.

As mentioned previously, we have discovered in some instances that the parents needed deliverance more than their child. They may need to be delivered even before the child, in order to be able to offer the child a stable family unit. Every child needs a stable home if he or she is to develop a stable personality. Stability becomes even more important if one parent is absent.

The parent's stability is a factor of primary importance, to prevent the child being reopened to demonic attack. That is, if there are problems in the home, they should be resolved before the child is delivered, if at all possible, lest the child be thrown back into the same situations that initially caused the problems.

Many times we have been contacted by grandparents who wanted to sneak a grandchild in for deliverance while they were babysitting, because the parents were not believers. We were opposed to it. Although opinions may differ, I don't have much faith for such deliverance. There may be exceptions, but this normally isn't a healthy procedure, because the child — even if totally delivered — will be returned to the environment that has produced the initial demonic problems, and will be without support.

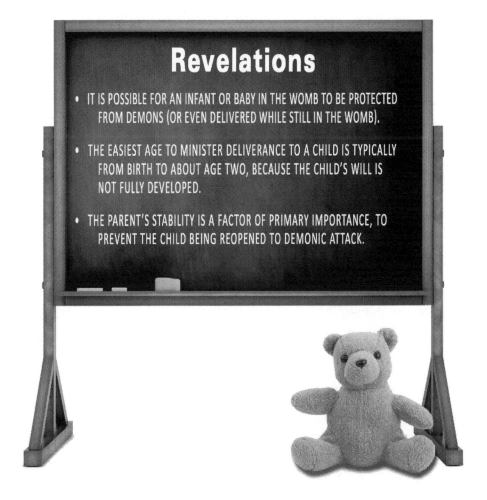

Revelations

- IT IS POSSIBLE FOR AN INFANT OR BABY IN THE WOMB TO BE PROTECTED FROM DEMONS (OR EVEN DELIVERED WHILE STILL IN THE WOMB).

- THE EASIEST AGE TO MINISTER DELIVERANCE TO A CHILD IS TYPICALLY FROM BIRTH TO ABOUT AGE TWO, BECAUSE THE CHILD'S WILL IS NOT FULLY DEVELOPED.

- THE PARENT'S STABILITY IS A FACTOR OF PRIMARY IMPORTANCE, TO PREVENT THE CHILD BEING REOPENED TO DEMONIC ATTACK.

26.
THE STAGES OF DELIVERANCE

It is a good practice to lead the child in a prayer such as the following:

> "Lord Jesus, I am sorry for all the bad things I have done. Please forgive me. I love You; I belong to You, and I want to live with You. I forgive everybody who has hurt me, made me mad, or made me cry. I forgive my mother and my father (if appropriate) and other people for _____. Now, I ask You to make the little skunk that causes me to fear (or do wrong things) to get out of me, in Jesus' name. Amen!"

The one ministering should then take authority over the spirits involved, and command them to leave.

It is also a good procedure to have the child sit facing you when you are ministering so that you can be able to see their face. This permits you to be able to detect reactions to your prayers. Experience has shown that the Lord often grants discernment to the ones ministering as they observe the facial reactions of the child.

It is a common practice for us and the parent(s) to hold the hands of the child being delivered. This will sometimes give an indication of the strength of the demon's hold and of his activity. The demon will often cause the child to fight to remove your hand and to resist your touch. In some instances a child will cry and try to prevent anyone from praying for him, even without any touch. The physical touch is a point of contact and has great power. Demons respond with hatred toward prayer, praying in tongues, and the Name of Jesus.

My wife once had an experience when a young boy fell off his bike and scraped his leg not far from her. She called to him and said, "Come here, and let me help you."

The crying child stood up, took one look at her and said, "No way! You're not going to pray for me!" and took off running.

His supernaturally knowing what was in her mind and fearing her touch or prayer was evidence of a spiritual stronghold.

You may encounter other symptoms during the deliverance. You may be led during the actual deliverance session to explain in terms the child can grasp, "Just open your mouth and let the little skunk come out; just like you open your mouth and take in a deep breath of air, blow him out. The skunk has to have a way to get out of you, so you open your mouth."

The child may become totally silent and still, almost like a small animal hoping to hide. He also may seem to become withdrawn, in another attempt to ignore the one ministering (hoping to be ignored in return). He might appear angry, or even become furious with rage. Counter his reactions with loving compassion. My experience has been that in true deliverance, the Lord usually gives the one ministering a supernatural compassion and love for the candidate, no matter how abusive the spirits within them may become.

DURING THE DELIVERANCE

It is important to reassure the child as the deliverance progresses, especially if there is resistance. Let the child know that you, the one ministering, recognize that it is not the child, but the little skunk that is causing the unpleasant manifestations. The child may begin to look as if he or she might cry. If so, then explain, "You may feel like crying while we're praying for you, and that is perfectly fine. It isn't you, it's the little skunk that is crying."

When the child is given directions such as these, the response can reveal to the one ministering the degree of cooperation that exists with the child. For instance, if you tell the child, "Open your mouth, take a deep breath, and then let it all out," and the demonic spirit is manifesting, it may cause the child to respond with a flat, "No!" In other cases the child may simply shake his head in refusal, and firmly clench his teeth or clamp his mouth shut, each of which reveals demonic resistance at work.

The one praying may be led to pray and command the spirit that's holding the mouth shut to loose its hold. It is the Holy Spirit's anointing that breaks the yoke, and our sensitivity to the Spirit is of prime importance. Always minister in love.

THE WILL OF THE CHILD

A common question is "How do you get through to the will of a child, or break the resistance of his or her will?" This is accomplished by the anointing of the Lord, by means of the gifts of the Spirit, through the discerning of spirits, the word of knowledge, and the word of wisdom. We have found that when God has prepared the individual, the deliverance flows naturally and easily. Experience and knowledge of deliverance are helpful, but recognize that we all start from the point of having had no experience, even as the Apostles did!

With older children, the will becomes involved; they can choose to keep the demon or reject it. We certainly do have authority over the evil spirits, and have parental influence over our children. We do not have authority over the fully-formed will of a child.

Be very loving in your attitude toward the child, but equally firm with the demon. I usually try to vary between speaking softly with the child, and giving firm commands to the skunk. This is a good practice to follow with adults also. Softly speak Scriptures or loving words of encouragement to the person, and then again speak firmly and authoritatively to the demon.

HOW DO WE KNOW WHEN THE CHILD IS DELIVERED?

How can we tell when a child is delivered? Sometimes the child will be able to tell you. It should become clear when the child either becomes relaxed and at peace, or the one ministering feels relaxed and observes an absence of the pressure that often accompanies deliverance. Such pressure is probably a gentle corollary to the pressure being exerted upon the demons by the Holy Spirit from within you. You might choose to think of it as a tensed muscle within you, holding one end of a spiritual stick or spear with which the Holy Spirit is routing the evil spirit.

Sometimes it will take a period of time to determine just how much the Lord has done in the child. This is particularly true when there have not been manifestations during the deliverance, which may often be the case. *Many deliverances result in little or no manifestation.* In other cases there will be immediate, observable symptoms that the deliverance has been effective. You may see the child who was very restless and irritable a few moments earlier, suddenly become peaceful when the deliverance is complete. Whereas before he was pouting or sad, after the deliverance he is bubbly and happy.

However, do remember that children differ. One may be very vocal, another can be very quiet. On a personal note, for years we thought our second son was never going to be able to speak because his older brother did all his talking for him. The older would look at the younger and say, "He wants water," or, "He wants a sandwich." We thought it was a great accomplishment when the younger finally would say, "Me too." When the older son asked for a cookie, or a piece of candy, our younger one would say, "Me too."

The point to be noted is to not expect each child to react in the same way. It is not terribly important whether we understand exactly how or when the deliverance has taken place. We can simply trust that the deliverance prayers have been heard, and that the Great Deliverer is on the case — even after the deliverance session has ended.

POST DELIVERANCE CONVERSATION

Following deliverance prayer, it is a good idea to thank and compliment the child, to congratulate him or her for helping in the process of chasing out the "little skunks." Just as you don't want to be rushed or crowded for time while engaging in deliverance, you also want to take the time to close the doors against Satan's reentry. Our goal in closing the session is to leave the child grateful to God for His help, understanding that Jesus will never leave or forsake him or her, and to be excited to go on with life in Him.

The post-deliverance ministry is important for the child. Assure the child that he or she is loved and accepted. Satan has been telling the child for a long time that if the parents were to find out about those sins, that they would hate or reject the child. Explain the lie behind Satan's threats, and make sure the child's parent(s) embrace the child.

If the child is old enough to understand, I offer suggestions to help the child continue to grow in his or her spiritual walk. It is important to instill in the child a sense of being on guard against future attacks of the enemy. The recommendations may be as simple as, "Come back if you start feeling any of these symptoms trying to return." I also like to give specific Scriptures to use in combating the child's particular area of weakness.

Emphasize to the child that Jesus is the light that has broken through the darkness, and Jesus has chased the little skunk away. It was His love that set him or her free.

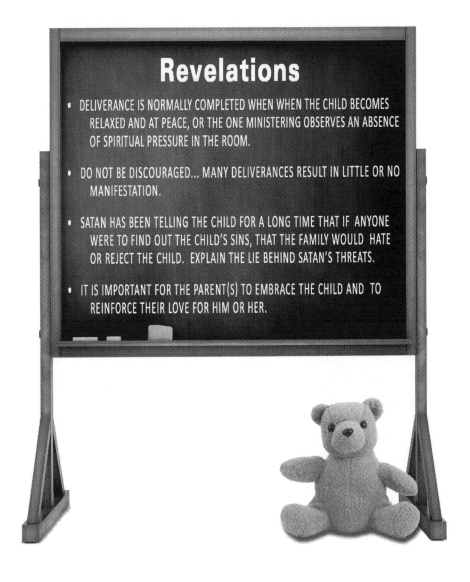

Revelations

- DELIVERANCE IS NORMALLY COMPLETED WHEN WHEN THE CHILD BECOMES RELAXED AND AT PEACE, OR THE ONE MINISTERING OBSERVES AN ABSENCE OF SPIRITUAL PRESSURE IN THE ROOM.

- DO NOT BE DISCOURAGED... MANY DELIVERANCES RESULT IN LITTLE OR NO MANIFESTATION.

- SATAN HAS BEEN TELLING THE CHILD FOR A LONG TIME THAT IF ANYONE WERE TO FIND OUT THE CHILD'S SINS, THAT THE FAMILY WOULD HATE OR REJECT THE CHILD. EXPLAIN THE LIE BEHIND SATAN'S THREATS.

- IT IS IMPORTANT FOR THE PARENT(S) TO EMBRACE THE CHILD AND TO REINFORCE THEIR LOVE FOR HIM OR HER.

It may also be important to break any generational curses off the family, and in particular, off the life of the child.

PRAYER TO BREAK A CURSE

"Lord Jesus: (1) I reaffirm you as my Savior and King, and I thank you for shedding Your blood for me, which cleanses me from all sin and allows me to become righteous in the sight of God. (2) I confess my sin or the sins of my ancestors that made my child eligible for this curse. I repent on my family's behalf, and ask your forgiveness for it. I ask for your help in righteously fulfilling my obligations to my child. By a decision of my will I break all ties with Satan, his kingdom, the occult or any other route of access that I or my family may have opened to him. (3) I acknowledge that you became a curse for me that I might be freed from all curses, and I now renounce and sever all ties with the curse of _____. I break its power over me, my family and my lineage, in your name and the authority of your completed work upon the cross. I ask You to cleanse my bloodline from it. (4) I thank you for having made provision for me in advance and for having broken this curse on the cross. In your precious name I pray. Amen."

DELIVERANCE FOR A CHILD'S ROOM, OR A HOUSE?

If the other forms of deliverance do not remove the tormenting problems from your child, another possibility does exist. Be sensitive to the Holy Spirit who may lead you to pray deliverance over the room in which your child sleeps, or even your whole house.

"Can my baby's room somehow be having an effect upon his personality?" a young mother recently asked me. "My grandmother committed suicide in the house where we are now living and my baby seems to be tormented. He can't seem to sleep through the night. I probably wouldn't have thought of it but a friend was having the same kind of problems with her children and she learned that a murder had previously taken place in her house. What can I do to rid my house of whatever kind of spirits may be lingering around?"

This question comes up frequently. "Can a building, or house, be inhabited by demons?" The answer is yes. So, too, can a piece of land, an occult book, an idol, a statue from a foreign country, or anything that has been utilized in some way in the worship of false gods. I have heard from Christian real estate professionals that potential customers, even those who were unbelievers, experienced a sensation of a cold chill and were repulsed by the presence of evil in a home on the market. One large estate had horrific child molestation and pornography filmed, and was finally bulldozed after two years of unsuccessful attempts to sell it.

It is always important to seek the Holy Spirit's guidance on such matters.[8] As to what can be done, the answer I would suggest is spiritual warfare. See if the Holy Spirit brings to mind any occult forces or sins of the current or prior residents. He may show you certain objects (or books and literature) that are occult, or remind you of something traumatic that happened in the home. I would recommend the following steps for a dwelling:

1.   Pray for the entire house or apartment, binding all spirits and commanding them to leave.

2.   Walk through the dwelling and pray over each individual room in the same fashion.

3.   Prayerfully ask the Lord to show you any objects that have been

8 You can also research more on the topic in the booklet, *Poltergeists - Demons in the Home.* by Frank Hammond. Impact Christian Books, Inc. **www.mpactchristianbooks.com/frank**

tainted by sin, or that are occult.

4. I like to dedicate to the Lord every building that I use (either rent or own) by praying and anointing at least the doorpost or threshold of the entry with oil. The oil is representative of the Holy Spirit, but in a greater sense, it is an act tied to the Israelites in ancient Egypt on the night of passover. The destroyer was unable to enter the homes which had the anointing of God (EXODUS 12). If the building is known to have an undesirable history, I would anoint the dwelling and dedicate it and its inhabitants to the Lord.

5. Some have felt led to sing praises to the Lord in each room. Worship in itself drives demons out of the atmosphere in a room and also binds them, as in the case of David and Saul (see 1 SAMUEL 16:23).

6. Others have felt led to have a prayer walk around the property, following the Scriptural example of the march around Jericho (see JOSHUA 6).

7. Some have felt it preferable to have others whom they respect, as mature in the Spirit, join them in these steps, which can help build faith.

There may be a need to remove tangible items from the baby's room. Such items may include monster toys, witch dolls or other frightening objects, anything of an evil appearance. Games like Ouija Boards or other occult or fantasy board games *attract* demonic spirits — there have been numerous cases in the news of entire groups of children being attacked by demons after playing these types of games. In addition, tainted objects may include things such as decorations composed of actual weapons, swords, spears or guns. Occult objects, or objects of other religions, can also attract demons. These include idols, like little Buddhas, good luck emblems, witch decorations, indigenous art or memorabilia, hex symbols, such as the all-seeing "eye of god," the Pennsylvania Dutch hex symbols, and anything else about which you feel uneasy. Books about reincarnation, false religions, or the occult are also strong candidates for elimination of evil spirits. The most important thing is to endeavor to be obedient to the directions which the Lord may impress on you rather than to follow a particular set of instructions. He might have you do something entirely different from the steps that I have suggested. Once the premises are cleansed, walk according to the instructions of the Lord to keep the doors closed to any further trespass by the enemy.

Revelations

- "CAN A BUILDING, HOUSE, OR APARTMENT BE UNDER THE INFLUENCE OF DEMONS?" THE ANSWER IS YES.

- SO TOO CAN A PIECE OF LAND, AN OCCULT BOOK, AN IDOL, OR ANYTHING THAT HAS BEEN UTILIZED IN SOME WAY BY OTHER RELIGIONS, OR IN THE OCCULT.

HELPING THE CHILD RETAIN DELIVERANCE

Deliverance must be maintained once it is accomplished. A stable, God-fearing, God-honoring household is one means of doing that. Probably the most important reason for ministering deliverance to children is that the vast majority of spirits encountered in adults were acquired during childhood. Children are especially vulnerable to the invasion of evil spirits.

Parents need to learn how to protect their children from receiving evil spirits; how to deliver their own children if they do have spirits; and then how to help keep them free from those spirits; that is, to maintain their deliverance.

If the child is very small, the responsibility remains of the parents. If the child is old enough, teach him or her to memorize Scriptures can be used to resist the enemy. Teach him or her to avoid — or flee — from sources of occult or temptation. The parents, regardless of the age of the child, have a responsibility:

- ➤ To be a spiritual covering for the child

- ➤ To protect the child from harm

- ➤ To pray for the child, to bless him or her with the favor of the Lord

- ➤ To bind any spirits that would try to come against the child

It is not always possible to prevent a child from being wounded, but a parent can be a buffer against those wounds. Don't let anyone mistreat your child: don't permit him or her to be shamed, or abused verbally, mentally, physically, or sexually. **We do our part in the natural, and petition God to do His part in the supernatural.** The parent has a role; the child has a role, and God has a role in keeping the child safe and free.

Daycare and Other Babysitting Situations

Daycare centers are an unfortunate fact of life confronted by many single or working parents. The selection of one should be given prayerful consideration. The child who cries when being dropped off at his daycare center may be indicating a problem.

The tears may reflect that the child does not want to be away from the mother, or there may be insecurity in the child. We understand that separation anxiety is a reality with any child.

However, the problem may exist within the daycare center itself. If the child is delivered from anxiety and still cries when taken to the day care center, the parent needs to examine the care given at the center. Sometimes, the demons in one child can affect the sense of protection and security of the other children at the center. In other more rare cases, the adults themselves are not suited to be caregivers for children.

We have been informally consulted in connection with some of these cases, to confirm the suspicions of authorities, that certain activities described by very small children were indeed part of satanic rituals or practices of witchcraft. The enemy certainly is no gentleman and will attack the most vulnerable whenever the opportunity arises, and he can find depraved men or women to do his bidding. Much prayer and attention should be given whenever a child is to be cared for by another adult.

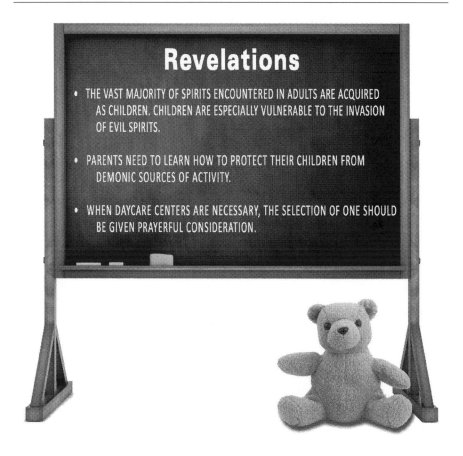

DELIVERANCE FROM PHYSICAL CONDITIONS

Some physical infirmities respond to deliverance. This does not mean all physical issues are demonic in nature. However, Jesus makes it clear in a number of scriptural examples that healing and deliverance may be intertwined:

> And, behold, there was a woman which had a *spirit of infirmity* eighteen years, and was bowed together, and could in no wise lift up herself. And when Jesus saw her, he called her to him, and said unto her, Woman, thou art loosed from thine infirmity. And he laid his hands on her: and immediately she was made straight, and glorified God.
>
> LUKE 13:11–13 [ITALICS MINE]

> As they were going out, a mute, demon-possessed man was brought
> to Him. After the demon was cast out, the mute man spoke; and the
> crowds were amazed...   MATTHEW 9:32–33, NASB

> "Teacher, I brought You my son, possessed with a spirit which makes
> him mute... He [Jesus] rebuked the unclean spirit, saying to it, "You
> deaf and mute spirit, I command you, come out of him and do not
> enter him again."   MARK 9:17–25, NASB [BRACKETS MINE]

If the child, for instance, has a problem with asthma, in addition to seeking medical help, pray against disorders of the lungs and respiratory system and trouble with the heart. Our oldest child "grew out" of asthma, although we think deliverance and healing by Jesus played a major role. If the child is frequently troubled with swollen glands, pray against susceptibility to sickness — and include binding the spirit of cancer, as a *preventative* form of prayer. If your child has allergies, as many do, pray against these as well. Our youngest child "grew out" of an allergy to dairy, and we were told by the consulting physician this was unlikely, if not impossible. Again, we prayed both deliverance and healing prayers for him. Whether it was a healing, or a healing through deliverance, we do not know.

The point is to always pray for the child's physical condition, while operating in the guidance of the Holy Spirit, and while working with medical professionals. Speak the blessing over your child on a consistent basis, that he or she is "fearfully and wonderfully made" (Ps. 139:14).

If the child is prone to be fearful or anxious, either pray silently when the child is asleep, or out of his or her hearing. We want to be on guard against planting seeds of additional fears in the child. Our goal is to get to the root issue behind the condition without creating fear within the child.

GOD'S BASIC POWER TOOLS FOR LIFE'S PROBLEMS

There are certain techniques which God has given us to help deal with the problems that confront our lives. He has provided what I like to think of as "God's Basic Power Tools," which should be explained and taught to a child. These are:

1. To confess sins

2. To forgive all others

3. To love in spite of wrongs, as in The Golden Rule: Do unto others as you would have others do unto you

4. To get rid of anger, bitterness, resentment or wrath.

"A wrathful man stirreth up strife: but he that is slow to anger appeaseth strife."   PRO. 15:1, 18

"Be ye angry, and sin not: let not the sun go down upon your wrath: Neither give place to the devil."   EPH 4:26–27

Deliverance is *not* a magic wand. It does not offer a solution to all life's problems. It is definitely not a substitute for discipline of one's children. Nor does it remove the necessity for future discipline and deliverance. One must still love the child enough to discipline, and one must also still love the child after having been delivered, when he or she may manifest unlovable behavior. Don't despair. Remember, God doesn't give up on His own! He did not give up on you!

"Even the captives of the mighty man will be taken away, and the prey of the tyrant will be rescued; for I will contend with the one who contends with you, and I will save your sons [and daughters]."
ISA. 49:25, NASB [BRACKETS MINE]

"It would have been easier to deliver my child when he (or she) was young. But my child is now a teenager. I have come to understand about salvation and deliverance. How can I introduce the subject of salvation and deliverance?"

PART FOUR
DELIVERANCE FOR TEENS

I HAVE NO GREATER JOY THAN TO HEAR THAT MY CHILDREN WALK IN TRUTH.   3 JOHN 1:4

BY FAITH JACOB... BLESSED BOTH THE SONS OF JOSEPH; AND WORSHIPED, LEANING UPON THE TOP OF HIS STAFF.   HEB. 11:21

"EVEN THE CAPTIVES OF THE MIGHTY MAN WILL BE TAKEN AWAY, AND THE PREY OF THE TYRANT WILL BE RESCUED; FOR I WILL CONTEND WITH THE ONE WHO CONTENDS WITH YOU, AND I WILL SAVE YOUR SONS [AND DAUGHTERS]."   ISA. 49:25, NASB [BRACKETS MINE]

DELIVERANCE
FOR TEENS

If the young child does not receive sound discipline accompanied by appropriate ministry at an early age, he may become a troublesome, rebellious teenager. Deliverance for an older teen is really no different than deliverance for an adult (as described in the book *Power for Deliverance*). The techniques for ministering to the teenager would be basically the same as those presented in our other books for adults.

27.
SALVATION

It is important to pray for **salvation** prior to deliverance. The extra freedom teens enjoy can be occasions for further demonic bondages, *unless* the teen has committed himself or herself to Christ.

Depending on the maturity of a teenager's will, the situation as a parent may be easier, or more difficult, than others. It really depends on the teen. However, there is a God-ordained, spiritual authority that a father and mother retain in a teenager's life, while they are "under their roof" so to speak, a spiritual authority that can be exercised on their behalf even if the teenager is resistant to salvation and deliverance. In the case of a rebellious and wayward teenager, you can still pray effectively for them through intercessory prayer warfare, when they are not in your presence. You can still have a major spiritual impact on their lives!

It is important to first understand your spiritual authority in Jesus Christ, and to second, to understand your spiritual authority as a parent, and third, to stand in that spiritual authority. Before anything happens on earth, it is accomplished in the heavenlies first

— in the atmosphere above your home and your child. If you do not have a conceptual basis for this authority, pray and ask Jesus to show you where you stand in terms of kingdom authority. Search out scriptures that confirm this authority to you.

Our battles in life, and within our families, are not against flesh and blood, but against the powers *behind* the flesh and blood. The issues of life become easier to deal with once the spiritual strongmen have been bound and minimized. In the case of a rebellious teenager, you can still pray effectively for him or her, even if they reject the Gospel, and your prayers will have a major spiritual impact on their lives.

28.
BAPTISM IN THE HOLY SPIRIT

Ideally, the *Baptism in the Holy Spirit* should be sought by the adult prior to ministering to their teen. Then, ideally, this baptism should be explained to the teenager.

The earlier this empowerment of the Holy Spirit is explained to a child the better, since wills can become hardened toward the subject as a child matures into a teen. Too much pressure, though, can get in the way of ministry. The teenager should be encouraged to read up on the subject and to seek further ministry. In some cases, simply receiving salvation or the baptism in the Holy Spirit *resolves* what was perceived as a need for deliverance.

29.
EXPERIENCED DELIVERANCE WORKER

By the time a child has reached the teen years, patterns of behavior and the relationship with his parents have usually been well established. Thus, unless there has been a history of effective prayer ministry with the child, and the teen has learned to completely trust his parents' prayers, it may be more effective to seek out an *experienced deliverance minister* in whom the parents have confidence. Ideally this should be someone with whom the family has had a long-standing relationship of trust, such as a pastor or close friend. Choosing someone outside the family is helpful if the child is already rebelling against the parents' authority. Through a third party, the teenager may be more open and receptive to truths from Scripture, and also ministry from the new source.

A TEEN CAN SEEK DELIVERANCE FOR HIMSELF (HERSELF)

It was noted earlier that a child raised with exposure to deliverance will learn to seek it for himself or herself when it is needed in later life.

Sam, a senior in high school, called one day sounding slightly embarrassed, but seeking an appointment for prayer and deliverance. His parents had told me previously that they were at their wits' end with him. He was not having any real problems in his life, but even his unbelieving girlfriend had recognized his need for help, and had suggested that he call to make an appointment for deliverance. Sam was having difficulty controlling his temper, which could flare at the slightest inconvenience or frustration.

When Sam arrived at our prayer room, he explained, "I don't know what's the matter with me. I'm having a terrible problem with my temper. I've been blowing up at everyone around me. I've been yelling at the people I love, and there really isn't any reason for it that I can think of. I need help."

Sam had always had difficulty grasping mathematical concepts due to a learning disability. He had been tutored from grade school on, and was now in trigonometry, and floundering. I asked if the frustration was greater now that he was in "trig." He said, "No, trig is frustrating, but it is no worse than other math all along."

After some explanation of deliverance, we then, in agreement, commanded the spirits that caused Sam to be short of temper, and explosive in anger, to manifest themselves, name themselves, and to come out. I also commanded any spirit of anger from being ridiculed by classmates, friends or teachers for his math learning disability to come out.

Although there weren't any violent manifestations, Sam did begin to sweat profusely. When we were through, he said, "I really do feel better already. I feel quiet and at peace deep inside." The entire prayer session had only taken about thirty minutes, from start to finish.

Often, when teenagers (or adults) come for deliverance properly prepared, and sufficiently desperate, they have already received a good portion of their deliverance beforehand, and do not have significant manifestations during the actual deliverance session. They have persevered by exercising their wills. Overcoming the resistance to making the call to set up the appointment, and the enemy's attempts to prevent them getting to the prayer room, can be the persistence needed to obtain the victory. Sam apparently had won a major part of his battle prior to coming in to see me for prayer.

I was, however, somewhat disappointed that there had not been a more obvious manifestation, for Sam's benefit. I felt that he would have been more sure of his deliverance if there were some form of manifestation, some visible sign of closure. However, I had learned long before that visible manifestations are not necessary for complete deliverance, and Sam did not seem the least bit disappointed.

His mother called the next afternoon to thank me for praying with Sam. She reported that he seemed a totally different person, that he had been listening to songs of praise all day, and had thrown out the few rock songs that he owned. A week later Sam himself called to thank me, to report that all was going well and that he had just gotten his first ever "A" on a math test, and in trigonometry nonetheless! A year later, I overheard his mother give a tearful and joyful testimony about the fantastic changes which God had worked in Sam. "Although he had always been a good kid, he has become so much more peaceful, and sweeter. He has become more bold in witnessing, too, and has even begun sharing his testimony publicly through a young people's organization in connection with his church youth group."

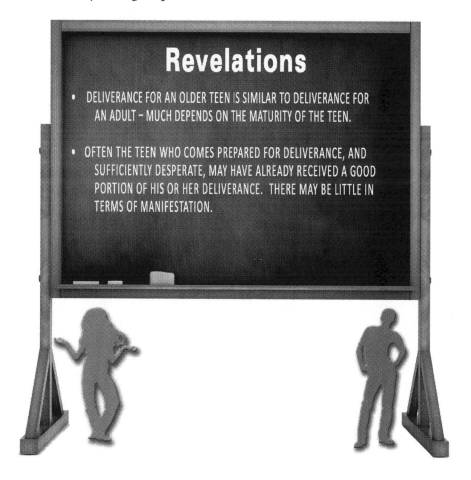

Revelations

- DELIVERANCE FOR AN OLDER TEEN IS SIMILAR TO DELIVERANCE FOR AN ADULT – MUCH DEPENDS ON THE MATURITY OF THE TEEN.

- OFTEN THE TEEN WHO COMES PREPARED FOR DELIVERANCE, AND SUFFICIENTLY DESPERATE, MAY HAVE ALREADY RECEIVED A GOOD PORTION OF HIS OR HER DELIVERANCE. THERE MAY BE LITTLE IN TERMS OF MANIFESTATION.

30.
UNIQUE NEEDS AMONG TEENS

There are certain areas of *unique needs* encountered in ministering to teens. Joan, an adult child of an alcoholic came seeking help, and I learned several things from her description of her teen years.

JOAN'S CASE: ADDICTIONS & COMPULSIONS

Having made an appointment, Joan came to visit our prayer room on the verge of tears. "I don't want to sound like I'm being critical of my parents because I love them both. And they are both really wonderful people. But I have to tell someone and get this off my chest or I think I'll go crazy."

"The problem that I have is," tears filling her eyes as she began, "I resent my father for his drinking. He can't help it and doesn't believe that he has a problem. Denial of the problem is one of our family's biggest problems. He refuses to see it, my mother won't admit it or face it, and my brothers and sisters normally won't talk about it either. I can't criticize my mother, she has kept the family together and she has worked hard to keep us in food and housing when my father drank up the rent money."

When she paused for a breath and to wipe away the tears with a tissue, I asked. "Do you have a fear of the family falling apart, or of him abandoning you?"

"Yes. We prayed against the fear of *abandonment* the last time I was here, and you also cast out a spirit of *anorexia nervosa*. You may recall I was a borderline anorexic when I was in my teens at college, which you said could be tied to my relationship with my father." She repeated herself, "I do love him, but at times I not only resent him… I think I even hate him for what he has done to our family. I am so angry with him, and so disappointed in him as a father for all the times he has embarrassed us. My whole family has been ashamed about the way he has acted at times. He let his kids down when he did not show up for functions at school, especially in my teen years." Joan finished with a huge sigh.

"Well, perhaps we should pray then about the ways he has failed both you and your family, and forgive him for failing to be the kind of father that you wanted and needed," I suggested.

"That's right, and there's still something more. I know that I need to be delivered of selfishness. I know my parents spoiled me:

my mother did it to make up for my father's failures. My father himself tried to make it up to me by giving us 'things.' As a result, I know I wasn't disciplined properly and was allowed to become self-indulgent, spoiled, rebellious and," Joan finally sobbed it out, "prideful." She continued, "I know I should not have it and I hate it, but I have a *spirit of pride*."

Joan sobbed in repentance and then broke the silence, "Before we pray, there's also something else that's kind of weird. It seems that every man that I date turns out to be wild, with alcoholic tendencies, or is already an alcoholic. I don't understand it. But I want to get rid of that too, if we can."

"Let me summarize and try to make some sense out of all this before we pray, okay?" I suggested.

"Sure. Please do," she replied.

"First, we recognize that you have feelings of resentment toward your father for his alcoholism and for all the ways he has failed you and your family over the years, and you need to forgive him. You also need to forgive your mother for not being able to protect you from your father's weaknesses, and for living in denial." Joan nodded silently in agreement.

I continued, "You have had a problem with compulsive behavior, and you've also recognized that your parents spoiled you attempting to compensate for the problems in the household. You have a fear of the family falling apart, a fear of losing your father through divorce or through death from alcohol abuse. You have anger against him, I think, because of a fear that he was committing suicide by drinking." Joan again nodded quietly.

"You know that you should love and honor your parents and are being tormented because you believe you are not doing so. Recognize this truth: we hate the sin but love the sinner. You love your parents and give them respect, but that doesn't mean you have to love your Dad's drinking."

We then prayed. She forgave her father and her mother, and confessed her sins "in the presence of a witness." We followed this by casting out the demonic spirits which we had uncovered, one by one. I then felt it appropriate to explain to Joan about a Christian being cleansed from sins.

"If you have a set of silver at home, you know how valuable silver is. But silver, in spite of its value, tarnishes. It is a precious substance exposed to a hostile environment, the air, and because of its contact with the environment, it tarnishes. It is still the same silver, still has the same value, but it appears dirty, and needs to be cleaned."

"The solution is to get out the silver polish and apply it with a little elbow grease, and soon the silver looks as good as new. This is a picture of us as Christians: we too are of great value and precious, but as we come in contact with a hostile environment, the world and its pollution of sins, we become tarnished. We feel dirty because of the sins that so easily rise against us, and we have to go to Jesus for cleansing. The blood is His cleansing agent which removes from us the taint, or tarnish of sin."

> "But if we walk in the light, as he is in the light, we have fellowship one with another, and the *blood of Jesus Christ his Son cleanseth us from all sin*... If we confess our sins, he is faithful and just to forgive us our sins, and to cleanse us from all unrighteousness."　　　　　1 JOHN 1:7,9 [ITALICS MINE]

LIKE FATHER, LIKE SON (OR DAUGHTER)

As Joan and I were talking, I realized why deliverance ministers hear so often "like father, like son." We hear adults often say, "I hate the way my father acted and the things he did, but now I am becoming the way he was and I am doing the same kinds of things he did." And from women the cry "I don't understand it, but I always date men who are alcoholics like my father!"

"Like father, like son." I have wondered for years why this is true.

The reasons are varied and complicated, but when viewed from the standpoint of spiritual warfare and spiritual roots, they become discernible. There are **five reasons** I can see:

1. The teen child of an alcoholic often picks up the same kind of addictive spirit that the father had either through *inheritance*, or by means of *acceptance*.

Acceptance is what occurs when the child learns a particular negative trait from a parent or other source and considers it to be an acceptable form of behavior. In order for this to change, the teen must fall out of agreement with the acceptance of the behavior.

Another example would be the individual whose parents had solved their marital problems by divorce. The spirit of divorce can run through a family for generations. Since there has been family contact with divorce, the stigma or the resistance to divorce does not exist. Thus the individual may consider divorce an acceptable solution for dealing with the problems of a marriage.

2. The addictive spirit functions in the teen the same way it functioned in the parent; the substance becomes a means of escape from problems. This is also a learned behavior, and *alcoholism* and *escapism* are intertwined. This is where "preventative deliverance" can play a very important role in a child or teen's life. **It is important to break a spirit's hold on the child or young adult as a preventative action, even though there may not yet have been any manifestations of that particular spirit or addiction at their age.**

3. The problem in the teen may have come from either parent, either the father who was alcoholic or the mother who was living in denial. The son, as mentioned above, may acquire an alcoholic spirit, while the daughter may receive from the mother a spirit that causes her to want to "save" or "mother" an alcoholic.

The daughter may be drawn to men with alcoholic tendencies because their personalities remind her of the lost chances to connect with her father. She may have a desire to mother the man, because she desires to be able to prevent her marriage from having the kind of problems she experienced in her childhood.

4. There may be a curse at work within the family. In this case, it would be *alcoholism*. It could also be related to a curse of *poverty*, since alcohol drains the family's finances. Along the same lines, the curse could be related to *loss of manhood*, since the father has for some deeper reason abdicated his role as a man and a father in the family. The solution to each and every curse is to break its power over the individual, and then to break it in the family lineage — over teens, children and grandchildren.

5. Becoming preoccupied with, or obsessive about, a wound experienced in one's teenage years can result in a subconscious replaying of that behavior.

In the cases of a teen with an addicted parent, the *fear of poverty* may be present in the teenager. The teen understandably fears that there will not be enough money for food, rent, and clothing. Perhaps he or she has heard the mother express her own fears, or the teen observes or experiences the lack firsthand. Even in cases where there has been no deprivation, the teen can have the fear that needs will not be met.

Many adults who have grown up as children or teens in alcoholic homes, and particularly those who are now Christians, may have feelings similar to Joan. They feel estranged from God the Father, and somehow failures in life. There can also be guilt from having resentment or hatred toward a parent(s), and not having properly forgiven them (MATT. 18:34).

The first step in the solution is to forgive the parents for failing to meet all the needs of their children.

PEER PRESSURES

In spite of the voices to be heard to the contrary, it is not necessary that every teenager go through a nasty rebellious stage, drink to excess, experiment with drugs, nor to become sexually active — even in college. I do not pretend that it is easy for the Christian teenager to resist peer pressure, but if it were not possible, what chance would the army of Christian soldiers have when engaging in other forms of spiritual warfare? What remnant is going to be around when the Lord returns? Resisting temptation has never been easy, but if one doesn't resist during the teen years, there is no indication one will be able in later life either.

Today so many of our young people have a hardened look about them. Why? It is, I suspect, because of incredibly early entrance of sin in their lives. The hard look is accentuated by eyeliner and makeup, as well as clothing and hairstyles. But if you look closely at the faces of these teenagers, especially the teenage girls, rather than the sweetness to be expected, too often you see a hardened, much older look. Many of these young people complain of being burned out on life, having experienced everything before many of us in the preceding generation even knew what life was all about.

An acquaintance who does a national teen radio show told me that there are over fourteen million teen prostitutes. Tragically, there are also millions of teen, unwanted pregnancies. The cause of all these problems is sin, including neglect or abuse by parents, or corrupted lifestyles of celebrity role models.

There are tremendous tensions and stresses for boys and girls in the dating environment, an environment fraught with the potential for rejection. In the teen years, self-doubts exist anyway. "Am I cute or handsome? Am I desirable? Does he/she like me?" There is great pressure exerted by peers to be acceptable socially, by doing, acting, behaving in acceptable ways. This can lead to experimentation with drugs, alcohol and sexual promiscuity. The solution to all these problems resides in an even stronger pressure: the Holy Spirit — God's truth, righteousness and virtue — as well as the love by parents. A powerful antidote to the enemy and his pressures is to have the teen confess from the heart that he or she is fearfully and wonderfully made (Ps. 139:14).

Revelations

• RESISTING TEMPTATION IS NEVER EASY. IF ONE DOESN'T LEARN TO RESIST DURING THE TEEN YEARS, THERE IS NO INDICATION HE OR SHE WILL BE ABLE TO RESIST IN LATER YEARS AS WELL.

• TODAY SO MANY OF OUR YOUNG PEOPLE HAVE A HARDENED LOOK ABOUT THEM. WHY? IT IS, I SUSPECT, BECAUSE OF THE INCREDIBLY EARLY ENTRANCE OF SIN IN YOUNG PEOPLE'S LIVES.

Rejection by Social Groups or Opposite Sex

The spirits of rejection encountered by the teen may be either logical or illogical, resulting from actual instances of rejection or mere *perceptions* of rejection. A wise parent would be aware of both possibilities. The teen may be hampered socially by a *spirit of rejection* or a *rejection causing spirit*. Such things exist. Normal feelings of inadequacy, insecurity, fear of people and shyness can, depending on the teen, all be taken to an extreme and thus become demonic. Such spirits may be inherited, learned or taught, as well as acquired through personal trauma or experiences.

The Case of Jerry

In junior high school, my friend Jerry called a girl on the phone to ask her to go with him to a movie. I never learned exactly what she said to him, but her response, and the way she treated him on the phone, crushed him. From that time on, Jerry said he "would never call a girl on the phone again." He would only make a date if he could catch a girl alone at school and ask her in person. Later, in high school when the senior prom rolled around, he asked a girl in person.

That bad experience, and his reaction to it, resulted in an isolating fear of women. He felt different from other boys, and that contributed to his becoming a loner throughout his teen years. He became easy prey for Satan to convince him that he was homosexual.

How tragic, that no one had either the wisdom or the experience to pray with Jerry to remove the hurt of the experience and to prevent Satan's foothold in his life. Some of the earliest and most effective spiritual warfare can be waged on behalf of our children as we pray them through the traumatic situations that all humans are bound to experience. To pray protection for our children is wise, but there is a place beyond the preventive stage where we must engage the enemy, *praying out the fiery darts* and removing the painful splinters before the infection of bitterness, resentment, hatred, self-pity or other serious wounds to the spirit occur.

FRATERNITY REJECTION

While in my teens, at my college, one of my roommates was crushed when he did not receive an invitation to join the fraternity of his choice. I hurt for him in his grief. He was normally a sweet, jovial individual, but he was in tears on learning that he was not going to be asked to join.

He was subsequently invited to join as part of a "package deal" arranged so that the fraternity could get an individual whom they really wanted. To illustrate the fickleness of the college "rush system," the following year this "desired candidate" had transferred to another school, and my former roommate, condescendingly accepted in the "package deal," was selected as the organization's chairman. So in the long run he proved to be of far more benefit to the group than their priority candidate.

Those who do not join a fraternity or sorority are often spared from experiences for which they will later have to repent. They are also spared from experiences they will need to be delivered from as well. Fraternities and sororities are secret societies, and owe their basis for existence, to a certain degree, to a mystique of secrecy. We are told in Scripture to have nothing to do with the works of darkness or with things done in secret.

> For it is a shame even to speak of those things which are done of them in secret.   EPH. 5:12

The remedy, for adults, is to repent of the involvement in a secret society, and to sever all ties with the darkness and secrecy of the fellowship. We discuss more on this in our book, *Breaking Unhealthy Soul Ties*.

Secret societies usually have either direct roots or close parallels to the *occult*. Many fraternities, as was the case with the college fraternity I joined, derive their rituals from Freemasonry.

Suicide and Causes

Suicide has become one of the leading causes of death among youth. A variety of factors contribute to its increase. Considering this issue from the perspective of spiritual warfare and spiritual roots, we have at least some insight into the potential causes.

A child needs to be reassured that the parents' problems are the parents' problems, and that he or she did not cause them.

> ➤ "It is not your fault that your father is an alcoholic."
> ➤ "It is not your fault that your parents can't get along."
> ➤ "It is not your fault that your parents got a divorce."
> ➤ "It is not your fault that your mother is sleeping around."
> ➤ "It is not your fault that your father is a womanizer."

The importance of communicating these truths to the child cannot be overemphasized. Feelings of guilt and self-blame have been cited as contributing causes in teen suicides. These situations on their own do not mean teens are troubled. There is usually more happening in the shadows of the teenager's life and in his or her mind. Consider the following points:

1. Young people are experiencing more contact with, and contagion from, Satan's kingdom.

This includes false religious cults including eastern mysticism, as well as blatant occult practices. Music also plays a large part in the lives and moods of young people. Rock, heavy metal, electronic dance and rap music produced by drug influenced and demonically-inspired composers can have spiritual effects upon the hearers, over time. The effect that music can have upon a tormented individual, in the reverse, is to be seen in the scriptural account of David playing worship music for Saul.

> … David took an harp, and played with his hand: so Saul was refreshed, and was well, and the evil spirit departed from him.
>
> 1 Samuel 16:23

An intelligent, sophisticated Christian teenager confessed to me that he used music like a drug, to escape from reality. Do not be fooled — music and spirituality are often intertwined.

Modern children's games, like fantasy board games that encourage role playing as witches, warlocks, or wizards, or which involve invoking demons (whether seriously or not), make the players vulnerable to demonic attack. Self-destruction can be invited through involvement with such games. I recently met a family who related to me that their ten-year-old son told them he shot himself as a result of playing the game. The only explanation he could offer was, "Something just came over me. It wasn't me."

Teenagers on occasion will experiment with witchcraft as a means of expressing rebellion against parents and against religious authority. Satan's followers aren't concerned with why; they welcome all prospects. In fact, they aggressively seek new converts. We encountered a local coven that used sex, drugs and prostitution to lure young men, and to exercise control over them. Other experimentation with the occult such as séances, Ouija boards, tarot cards, chanting or meditation, levitation, hypnosis, fortune-telling, E.S.P., and horoscopes also open the unsuspecting teen to Satan's attacks — including self-destructive demonic spirits.

Satanism has become so real a threat today that the government has had to become involved. Special training sessions are being offered to representatives from local police departments on the characteristics of satanic rituals and abuse.

The press coverage given Satanic, cult, and mass murders attract national attention. All the terror we hear of on the news illustrates the flagrant ways in which Satan is rearing his ugly head and encouraging a self-destructive death cult in our country.

Revelations

- ROCK, HEAVY METAL, DANCE AND RAP MUSIC, PRODUCED BY DRUG INFLUENCED, DEMONICALLY-INSPIRED COMPOSERS CAN HAVE SPIRITUAL EFFECTS, OVER TIME, UPON THE HEARERS.

- CAREFUL ATTENTION SHOULD BE PAID BY THE PARENT TO THE LYRICS OF MUSIC TO WHICH THE TEEN LISTENS. MUSIC CAN BE A DOOR-OPENER FOR SELF-DESTRUCTIVE BEHAVIOR.

- TEENS ON OCCASION EXPERIMENT WITH WITCHCRAFT AS A MEANS OF EXPRESSING REBELLION AGAINST PARENTS AND RELIGIOUS AUTHORITY.

2. THE PRESSURES OF TODAY'S LIFESTYLES CREATE PROBLEMS FOR THE TEEN.

Some teens do not have a strong loving family, a good solid interactive neighborhood with friendly neighbors (who act like an extended family), and a church with active youth groups. This does not mean they are troubled, and some excel in the face of challenges. But the lack of a support network places a lot of pressure on the teen.

There are many fears and pressures that teens today experience. Things like nuclear war and mass terrorism are new to the most recent generations of teens. Hopelessness can reside inside a teenager who anticipates there being no future due to the environment, the economy, or the globalization of traumatic events broadcast through the media. If something bad happens at a neighboring school, you can be sure the news will be spread and be discussed among students, even the young ones, within a day or two.

Despair resulting from broken homes, or out-of-order homes, create additional stress among teens. Additional pressures are created by divorce, being torn between parents and the grief caused. Many teens complain of being unhappy or sad due to the family unit having been broken, or one parent absent.

Alcohol and drugs can become a form of escape for the teen, as they are more readily available. These means of escape only compound the situation. At the extreme end of such addictions, the number of teen overdoses from heroin is skyrocketing. Drugs may cause a teen to feel entrapped, that there is no chance of escape. When on drugs, a teen also experiences guilt, shame and the fear of discovery. Satan works in the shadows, and hates being exposed to the light. A teenager on drugs may also become increasingly manipulative, in order to hide the use or to obtain cash to support the habit. The teen-user may also suffer effects on brain chemistry.

Sexual pressure on teens is increasing as distortions of sex make more and more inroads into everyday life. Statistics were recently published stating that sex among teens is even worse than expected. Sixty-eight percent of teens from *conservative church backgrounds* admitted to having been sexually active. If those teens with a moral and Godly incentive chose not to be chaste, it is hardly surprising that the majority of teens outside the church complain of being sexually burned out. Their complaint, "Illicit sex is no longer a kick, why bother living?" Similarly, they are bombarded in our society with sexual stimuli and are exposed to sexual perversion, pornography online, homosexuality, lesbianism and masturbation. These have become, increasingly, a normal part of life.

Tragically, many have become addicted to pornography, which is easily obtainable. Sexual promiscuity and disease, coupled with the guilt of addiction to sex, greatly increases the pressure experienced by the teen.

There is also the "copy-cat" suicide syndrome which is more prevalent due to the speed and distance that news travels. There can become a contagion-like effect of suicide when school communities experience a suicide.

There are also many lures for teens to venture into unreality. They can have an unreal view of life and death caused by television or movies, or video games, which often portray death as a quick, painless or heroic end. They are lured into cyberspace, an alternative reality or a digital life. They may send or receive harsh comments online, known as cyber-bullying, which take a lie and amplify it to the surrounding community. Some teens take these lies to heart, and feel that their life is over.

CASE: MARY AND SUICIDE

Mary wanted to speak with me and ask for counsel. "Mr. Banks, my brother just recently committed suicide, and I find I don't want to live any longer myself. I always believed him to be a sincere Christian. He went forward two years ago and made a commitment to the Lord, and has faithfully attended church. He was an honor student, and a class officer at his high school. Did his suicide banish him to hell?"

"Mary, please don't take what I am about to say as in any way endorsing suicide. It is clearly wrong for anyone to take his life, especially for a Christian, whose body is considered to be the 'temple of the Holy Spirit.' But I am firmly convinced that *suicide* is a *demon* or an *evil spirit*. You and I cannot come to a logical conclusion to kill ourselves. We can only come to that conclusion if we are mentally ill, or under the severe torment of a demon." I paused and she nodded in agreement.

"If what I have just said is true, as I believe it to be, then I can see no more basis for God denying entrance to heaven for a victim of a *spirit of suicide*, than I can for one who died as a result of a *spirit of cancer*, or one whose death resulted from a battle with addiction. As I understand it, one's basis for entry into heaven is having believed and accepted Jesus' offer of adoption into the family of God, by accepting Him as Savior and Lord. Thus, irrespective of the manner of one's death, heaven awaits the true believer." This does not condone or make excuses for suicide, but it helps us better understand the spiritual forces at work.

It should also be noted that a *spirit of suicide* can be inherited through family lineage, and rear its head in the teen years. Just as spirits of *alcoholism* can pass from parent or grandparent to child, so too can more overt self-destructive spirits.

I happened to have on my prayer room table several articles containing interesting statistics on suicide among our youth which someone had just given me to read. I shared with Mary that the Centers for Disease Control in Atlanta, in a survey of 8th and 10th grade students, found that 34% of all the students had thought seriously about ending their lives. Fifteen percent had gone so far as to actually inflict injuries on themselves.

These figures agree with the overall statistics that show that 85% of all potential suicides did not really want to die. Most attempts were made at home during the evening hours when the family was available and present to prevent an attempt. The true cry of the potentially suicidal child is, "Notice me! Love me! I am unhappy and hurting!"

Mary experienced relief and we then prayed together, renouncing the *spirit of suicide* that had been attempting to harass her.

SUICIDE CAN BE HARD TO SQUARE WITH REASON

There may be a *spirit of rejection* and associated wounds at work in the troubled, suicidal teen. Repeated rejections can result in a form of *self-hate* — even if the teen is prospering in his school work or sports. Suicide may also involve mental illness, or chemical imbalances in the brain, not necessarily something demonic.

Self-mutilation, cigarette burns and razor cuts in the flesh ("cutting"), are an outward cry of "Help me! I hate this body. Something (or someone) is causing me to hate myself!"

One teen was a high school senior, captain of the football team, captain of the basketball team, in line to be valedictorian of his class and from a good Christian family, yet hanged himself. He left a note stating that the reason for it was that he had committed a sin, something so terrible that he was convinced it was unforgivable.

How tragic that Christians do not fully grasp forgiveness. Just as parents can love their teenager in spite of their shortcomings, failures and mistakes, so too can a loving and compassionate God love them, *to an even greater degree*, in spite of their mistakes.

There is, of course, a fine line between teaching children that they can be forgiven for anything by the Lord, and creating a mentality of license to do anything they wish (i.e. licentiousness). Children need to be lovingly instructed and trained — and warned of the dangers of drugs, illicit sex, experimenting with the occult and such.

"I don't care if I live or die," is a commonly heard response which reflects the conflict between the two opposing forces within troubled teens. The urge to preserve one's own life is countered by the frustration of unhappiness in life.

Psychiatrists have noted suicidal problems resulting from teens being associated with certain anti-social groups. Careful attention should be paid by the parent to the types of friends, and the lyrics of music to which the teen listens. Much of the music today is a door-opener for *self-destructive* behavior. Self-destructive behavior can also be learned through other teens at school.

There are symptoms to watch for, and you should consult with the teenager's physician for a more complete list:

Abrupt changes in personality, sudden mood swings, failure in school, changes in eating habits, becoming bulimic or anorexic (as described in *Deliverance From Fat & Eating Disorders*), morbid fears, fascination with death, sleep problems, abnormal sleeping (such as no sleep for days or sleeping around the clock), bullying, hopelessness, despair; the loss of someone or something very important in the teen's life... the death of a pet, the death of a member of the family, the death of the family itself through divorce, the death of a good friend or a good friend's parent; taking irrational or big risks, frequent serious auto accidents and the like, are all indications of a seriously troubled teen. The making of a will, giving away treasured possessions, along with changes in eating habits gives a warning to the family.

Alcohol and drug abuse can create instability in the mental processes; people on drugs, or who have experimented with drugs, may become impaired from rational thinking.

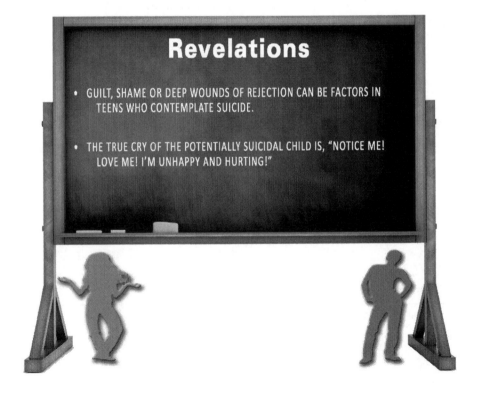

Revelations

- GUILT, SHAME OR DEEP WOUNDS OF REJECTION CAN BE FACTORS IN TEENS WHO CONTEMPLATE SUICIDE.

- THE TRUE CRY OF THE POTENTIALLY SUICIDAL CHILD IS, "NOTICE ME! LOVE ME! I'M UNHAPPY AND HURTING!"

31.
HOW TO PRAY WITH TEENS

When a teen comes for ministry, he or she may present a lesser, more socially acceptable problem, as a thermometer to "test the water." They are checking to see if the one ministering deliverance will be judgmental and rigid, or compassionate and loving. This is OK, and is a good place to start the ministry. As the deeper issues surface, it takes Spirit-anointed, prayerful discernment to determine whether the teen seeking deliverance is sincere.

It is often helpful to have the teenager read something on the subject of deliverance in advance to prepare himself or herself. The teenager should also be directed to prepare a list of problems or torments in advance, and to prayerfully determine that he or she wants to be free.

It is important for the teen (or adult) seeking deliverance to have a desire to be free from the tormenting spirit and to not be playing games — one should not be indecisive when dealing with the devil. The teen should be willing to be totally honest, at least with the one to whom he goes for ministry. One of the unfortunate aspects of deliverance ministry is that it *cannot be forced* upon someone. The teen, or adult, must be willing to be open and to be teachable in order to receive help.

It is helpful to establish — or re-establish — the direct relationship between the teen and Jesus. Often, teens coming for ministry have not had a good relationship with Jesus or felt worthy of such. It is good to open with a prayer of dedication or re-dedication where you tell the teen what to say. This opens the direct lines of communication between the teen and Jesus, through the presence of the Holy Spirit.

SAMPLE PRAYERS FOR TEENS

Below are sample prayers you can use to pray with your teen.

Be aware that this is a very special moment. What is about to take place is a transaction, between the teenager and Jesus. They give Jesus the bad stuff (the issues that torment them), and Jesus gives them the good stuff in return (peace, joy, and a sense of righteousness).

Respect the moment — do not rush through this prayer. This is a life-changing encounter with Jesus.

Have the teen repeat the words as you speak them:

"**Lord Jesus,**

I thank You for being present with me in this room right now. [pause to let this concept sink in].
I want to take this opportunity to thank You so much for loving me. [wait for the teen to identify with what they just said, and let the Holy Spirit confirm these words in his or her heart].

Today, Lord Jesus, I want you to know that I love You, too. [pause again, and wait for the teen to identify with these words, and to connect with Jesus in his or her heart. This is a powerful moment, do not rush it].

Jesus, take from me the things that cause me pain, the things that torment me, the things that make me feel bad about myself or cause me regret. [At this point, have them review the top 2 or 3 issues that are causing them trouble, either out loud, or if they are being shy, in their mind. This may take a minute, or longer, be led by the Spirit].

I now place those things in a box in front of me. I wrap that box with a big red bow, like a present, and I hand it to You, Jesus. [pause, give those words time to work in his or her heart].

I agree to surrender those things to You now, and I take my hands off them! Thank You for being willing to take them from me so I don't have to carry them with me anymore. [pause again, to let the words sink in].

I ask you to wash me as white as snow. Purify me.

Jesus, I invite you into my heart, and I surrender my life to You. [The prayer should be moving more smoothly now as the will of the teenager is in agreement with the environment of the Holy Spirit in the room].

Come into my life.
Talk with me, Jesus.
Walk with me.
Dine with me.
Hang out with me.
Be there when I wake up in the morning, and be there when I go to bed at night.

I thank you Jesus that you will never leave me or forsake me. I am your son [or daughter]. I am a child of the King. I receive your unconditional love, your never-ending love, now.

Amen!"

Now is a good time to lead the teen through a prayer of forgiveness. Have him or her forgive all those who have wronged them in any way, reminding them that Jesus has just done the same for them. Tell them that forgiveness is a door through which healing and deliverance flow. Here is a sample prayer of forgiveness:

"Lord Jesus, I confess and I am sorry for harboring unforgiveness inside of me. I realize that resentment and bitterness do not change a situation, they only serve to make it worse. I make the decision now to forgive my parents and _____, for hurting me by _____. I give up my right to be angry with them. I confess my bitterness and resentment as sin. I ask You to wash me as white as snow, by Your blood.

Now, by a decision of my will, I forgive those people who have wronged me, and I ask You to forgive them as well. I rebuke the poison in my body, mind and heart from holding murderous hate towards them. In Jesus' Name, Amen."

Having the teen void himself or herself of unforgiveness is a major step! This loosens any grip the enemy might have on them or their heart.

The next step is to break with any known sin, including experimentation with sex, drugs, self-harm, unrighteous music, and false religions including the occult. This is a more detailed prayer than the introductory one.

Have them verbally break any ties they can think of to darkness, or the demonic kingdom, through avenues of experimentation, etc.

Then, work with the teen to show them how to take authority over the spirit and to cast them out, reminding them that where two or more are in agreement concerning the Kingdom of God, Jesus is present in the room!

"In the name of Jesus Christ, I take authority over the spirit(s) tormenting me. I bind you... like an animal tied with ropes and chains. You spirit of _____, I fall out of agreement with you now.

I command the demonic source of torment to leave me right now. I am loosed in Jesus' name!

I chose to rest and recover, in the presence of the Holy Spirit.

Amen!"

32.
PRAYING FOR LOST TEENS

There are two opposite and extreme views that parents may have regarding deliverance: either nothing is demonic or everything is demonic. Avoid both extremes. Balance is needed, and so is love and sensitivity when introducing the subject of spiritual warfare to your teen. Keep in mind that the Lord has provided spiritual weapons for this battle, not fleshly ones.

All ministry and the gifts of the Holy Spirit work in an environment of love. This holds especially true in spiritual warfare. Your teen, like all of us, desires to be loved and accepted. So, remain consistent in your affection, remembering that the same love and concern that is motivating you to seek deliverance for him or her should be on display. Let your teen know how much you love and care for him or her. Give them unconditional love. Pray for the strength and ability to love *even more* than you currently do.

Do not let your anger at your teenager's problems cause you to treat him or her in an unloving way. Remember Paul's words in Ephesians 6, "We wrestle not against flesh and blood." Our warfare is not directed at the teen, but rather at the demons influencing the teen. So, do all in love. Love works wonders. Keep in mind that Scripture presents a balanced approach to parenting:

> Children, obey your parents in the Lord, for this is right. Honor your father and mother (which is the first commandment with a promise), so that it may be well with you, and that you may live long on the earth.   EPH. 6:1–3, NASB

And,

> Fathers, do not provoke your children to anger, but bring them up in the discipline and instruction of the Lord.
>
> EPH. 6:4, NASB

RECOMMENDED BATTLE STRATEGY

If the teenager is not open to salvation or deliverance, then parents can engage in **intercessory prayer warfare**. This binds the influence of demons. It exerts pressure on the spiritual forces blinding the mind of the young person from the truth and light of Jesus. This process may take time.

Pray specifically for your teen to receive *salvation* and the *baptism* in the Holy Spirit.

If there are specific areas of demonic activity that you recognize, such as *alcoholism* for example, bind that specific spirit in your intercessory prayer for your teen. Also bind any sicknesses, addictions and torments that have appeared in the generations. Utilize the two-fold weapons of praying with your understanding and praying in the Spirit. Both are powerful weapons that can serve in a defensive and offensive capacity. The intense opposition and resistance so often directed against *praying in the Spirit* bears adequate testimony that it has tremendous power.

To recap, the seven aspects of our spiritual battle plan for this tormented, unsaved teen:

1. Love your teen to the best of your ability, and pray for even more love; love him or her as Jesus loves you.

2. Don't let your anger be directed at your teen, but focus your righteous anger upon the demonic spirits;

3. Bind the spirits blinding his or her eyes to spiritual reality and the truth of the Gospel; Bind and keep on binding these spirits.

4. Pray for your teen to be saved and baptized in the Holy Spirit;

5   Pray against specific spirits if recognized, such as addictions;

6. Utilize prayer with your understanding; and

7. Pray in the Spirit for your teen

For parents of teenagers, there comes a time when having prayed in faith, you should rest from your efforts, trusting that the prayer has been heard, and that the answer has been dispatched and will be received. Prayer and fasting are powerful tools of intercession. One of our sons went through a period of about four years, during and after college, of being burned out in legalistic prayer groups. Then he again began to desire Christian fellowship, Christian Bible studies and to attend church functions. We knew that he was okay spiritually, even though we were concerned that he was not involved or "plugged-in" anywhere. But after that period of time, having been allowed the freedom to wait, rather than being forced into something, the hunger was restored. God does not give up on His own!

There is hope as Jane's story illustrates...

THE MIRACLE OF JANE GIVES US ALL HOPE

A tremendous example of the power of God to answer prayers beyond time and space is the story of Jane. It is a story that blesses me because it is a great example of God's provision, mercy, grace and *willingness* to save a soul in answer to a prayer, even the prayer of someone unknown.

A young woman, who had received the baptism in the Spirit in our prayer room, came to see me stating, "I know that I need some deliverance because of the wild past that I've had, and because of the things that I did in my teenage years."

Perhaps it was the way she had her hair that day. This day, when I looked at her, she seemed more familiar to me than at our first meeting. I asked her again, "Jane, haven't we met at some time in the past? You seem awfully familiar to me."

She said, "No, I don't think so, except for the time I came for the baptism in the Spirit a few months ago."

I thought for a moment. Then, the Lord brought back a memory He had me save from many years ago. It came to me, as in a vision. I asked her, "Have you ever been on *television?*"

She gave me a shocked look, and said, "Yes I was, but just one time."

As the picture in my mind became clearer, I asked if her one appearance on television was on a comedy show.

She replied with a strangely amused look, "Yes, but" she continued, "no one has ever told me they saw the show. If you saw it, you're the first person in all these years who has seen the show... from more than ten years ago!"

My mind was reeling as I continued, "Not only did I see it, but I can tell you exactly what took place on it! A famous comedian was appearing as a guest that evening on this popular, primetime T.V. show. The producers were going to have this comedic actor do body painting on a female model. You were that model. They were going to use *you* as the model. When you came out on stage you were in a yellow swimming suit, a bikini. As you came out, they asked your first name, and asked how tall you were."

She was absolutely stunned. "That's exactly what happened! How did you know? How do you remember it all so well?"

I continued, "Well, you won't believe this," as the shiver of the Holy Spirit ran down my spine. I related to her what had taken place in my living room some ten years before, when I saw her come out on stage on that program. I had sensed in my spirit that she didn't belong on that show; that she was totally out of place. I was led to pray that God would save her, get her out of that kind of lifestyle, and turn her life around!

Now here was Jane, more than ten years later, sitting in my prayer room, having been saved, baptized in the Spirit, a housewife and mother of several healthy children. God had not only answered my prayer, but done it beyond my wildest comprehension. Here sitting in my prayer room, in the middle of the country, was the answer to a prayer I had uttered 10 years prior for an unknown teen on a television show on the West Coast. God had even graciously allowed me to be an instrument in drawing a troubled teen into a relationship with Him. I am, to this day, astounded at the beauty and perfection of God's workings and answers to prayer.

With God all things are possible. This account stimulates our faith to believe God for the saving not only of strangers, but more so for the saving of our own, precious teenagers.

Jesus wants to encourage you to pray for your children and teens. If He could get Jane out of that kind of lifestyle, then He can certainly get your child out of drugs, alcohol, smoking, sexual problems or any other kind of undesirable link to the demonic kingdom.

May the Lord write on your heart the promise that:

Nothing is too difficult for our God!

A CHILD'S INTRODUCTION TO DELIVERANCE

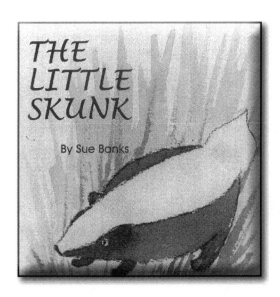

THE LITTLE SKUNK - A CHILD'S INTRODUCTION TO DELIVERANCE
BY SUE BANKS

A children's story **book** (or **e-book**)! For the child to read with a parent to understand the subject of deliverance without fear. Includes color illustrations to accompany the story, and assistance at the end for the parent to pray with the child. Watch how Charlie, Billy and Susie try to get the little skunk out of their house! (Deliverance need not be frightening if properly presented).   0892281200

A MANUAL FOR
CHILDREN'S DELIVERANCE
BY FRANK HAMMOND

This **book** (or **e-book**) for parents looking to minister to children is a valuable tool to learn how to set children free from spiritual bondages. Learn the basics of how to effectively minister deliverance to children, and the kinds of demonic influences prevelant in the child's world.

0892280786

MIRACULOUS TESTIMONIES
OF DELIVERANCE

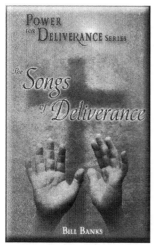

9780892280315

POWER FOR DELIVERANCE
THE SONGS OF DELIVERANCE   BY BILL BANKS

Learn that there is help for oppressed, tormented, and compulsive people, and that the solution is as old as the ministry of Jesus Christ. With 30 years of counseling and ministering deliverance, Bill Banks highlights the root causes of emotional and mental torment, and walks the reader through steps to be set free. Read numerous case studies of people who have been delivered from their torments and fears, including deliverance cases of over 60 spirits...

Ministering to Abortion's Aftermath
BY BILL & SUE BANKS

Millions of women have had abortions. Many were unaware of the physical, emotional and spiritual consequences, and still carry the trauma of the event with them - even years later.

In *Ministering to Abortion's Aftermath*, read a dozen real-life stories of women who have found deliverance and freedom from the various bondages associated with abortion, including emotional torment, physical complications, and more. Learn how their triumph can be yours.

9780892280575

Discover in this book (or e-book) the strategic steps and simple truths that have led these women, and hundreds more like them, to be set free. This book is full of hope - **hope that heals!**

Do Your Relationships Produce
Bondage or Joy?

Does someone manipulate you?
What are the symptoms of an ungodly relationship?
Are you tormented with thoughts of a former lover or friend?
Are you free to be all that God intended you to be?

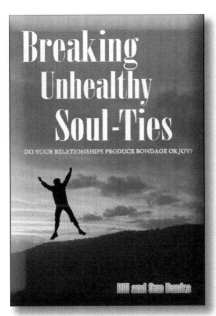

9780892281398

STUDY GUIDE 9780892282043

"Here at last is a thorough and theologically sound treatment of a little understood subject" - from the *Foreword* by Frank Hammond

BREAKING UNHEALTHY SOUL-TIES

BY BILL & SUE BANKS

Unhealthy soul-ties involve the control of one individual over another, and can be one of the most difficult blocks to spiritual freedom. Some relationships are healthy and bring blessings into our lives; other types of relationships can bring demonic bondage to our souls. This book and e-book assists the reader in diagnosing both healthy and unhealthy relationships, and offers positive steps to personal freedom.

FRANK HAMMOND BOOKS & EBOOKS

PIGS IN THE PARLOR 0892280271

A handbook for deliverance from demons and spiritual oppression, patterned after the ministry of Jesus Christ. With over 1 million copies in print worldwide, and translated into more than a dozen languages, *Pigs in the Parlor* remains the authoritative book on the subject of deliverance.

STUDY GUIDE: PIGS IN THE PARLOR 0892281995

Designed as a study tool for either individuals or groups, this guide will enable you to diagnose your personal deliverance needs, walk you through the process of becoming free, and equip you to set others free from demonic torment. Includes questions and answers on a chapter-by-chapter basis as well as new information to further your knowledge of deliverance.

OVERCOMING REJECTION 0892281057

Frank Hammond addresses the all-too-common root problem of rejection and the fear of rejection in the lives of believers, and provides steps to be set free. Learn how past experiences can influence our actions, and how we can be made whole.

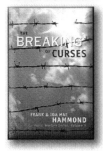

THE BREAKING OF CURSES 089228109x

The Bible refers to curses more than 230 times, and 70 sins that cause curses are put forth in Scripture. Learn how Curses are just as real today as in Biblical times. This book shows what curses are and how you may deliver yourself and your family from them.

A MANUAL FOR CHILDREN'S DELIVERANCE 0892280786

The Hammonds' book for ministering to children is a valuable tool for parents to learn how to set their children free from spiritual bondages. Learn the basics of how to effectively minister deliverance to children.

FRANK HAMMOND BOOKS & EBOOKS

CONFRONTING FAMILIAR SPIRITS
0892280174

A person can form and develop a close relationship with an evil spirit, willfully or through ignorance, for knowledge or gain. When a person forms a relationship with an evil spirit, he then has a familiar spirit. Familiar spirits are counterfeits of the Holy Spirit's work.

REPERCUSSIONS FROM SEXUAL SINS
0892282053

The sexual revolution has impacted our nation, our church and our family. Promiscuity, nudity and sexual obscenities have become commonplace. The inevitable consequence of defilement is the loss of fellowship with a holy God. Learn how to break free from the bondage of sexual sin.

THE MARRIAGE BED
0892281863

Can the marriage bed be defiled? Or, does anything and everything go so long as husband and wife are in agreement with their sexual activities? Drawing from God's emphasis on purity and holiness in our lives, this booklet explains how to avoid perverse sexual demonic activity in a home.

SOUL TIES
0892280166

Good soul ties covered include marriage, friendship, parent/child, between christians. Bad soul ties include those formed from fornication, evil companions, perverted family ties, with the dead, and demonic ties through the church. Learn how you can be set free from demonic soul ties.

OBSTACLES TO DELIVERANCE
0892282037

Why does deliverance sometimes fail? This is, in essence, the same question raised by Jesus' first disciples, when they were unable to cast out a spirit of epilepsy. Jesus gave a multi-part answer which leads us to take into account the strength of the spirit confronted and the strategy of warfare employed.

FORGIVING OTHERS
089228076X

Unforgiveness brings a curse, and can be a major roadblock to the deliverance and freedom of your soul. Find the spiritual truths regarding the necessity of forgiveness and the blessings of inner freedom which result!

AUDIO CDS

BY FRANK HAMMOND

AUDIO TEACHING SERIES

  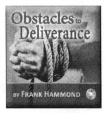 

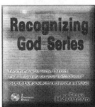   

BY FRANK HAMMOND

DVD VIDEOS

DVD TEACHING SERIES

 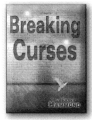  

* All DVDs are U.S.A. NTSC Standard

Watch & listen to excerpts now at:
www.impactchristianbooks.com/frank

Impact
Christian
Books

Website: WWW.IMPACTCHRISTIANBOOKS.COM

Phone Order Line: (314)-822-3309

Address: **IMPACT CHRISTIAN BOOKS**
332 LEFFINGWELL AVE. SUITE #101
KIRKWOOD, MO 63122

Made in the USA
Middletown, DE
13 February 2020

84764736R00115